Mindset Magic

Matthew Black

Square Reads

Copyright © 2023 by Matthew Black

The content contained within this book may not be reproduced, duplicated, or transmitted without direct written permission from the author or the publisher.

Under no circumstances will any blame or legal responsibility be held against the publisher, or author, for any damages, reparation, or monetary loss due to the information contained within this book. Either directly or indirectly. You are responsible for your own choices, actions, and results.

Legal Notice:

This book is copyright protected. This book is only for personal use. You cannot amend, distribute, sell, use, quote or paraphrase any part, or the content within this book, without the consent of the author or publisher.

Disclaimer Notice:

Please note the information contained within this document is for educational and entertainment purposes only. All effort has been executed to present accurate, up-to-date, and reliable, complete information. No warranties of any kind are declared or implied.

Readers acknowledge that the author is not engaging in the rendering of legal, financial, medical or professional advice. The content within this book has been derived from various sources. Please consult a licensed professional before attempting any techniques outlined in this book.

By reading this document, the reader agrees that under no circumstances is the author responsible for any losses, direct or indirect, which are incurred as a result of the use of the information contained within this document, including, but not limited to, — errors, omissions, or inaccuracies.

First Edition

ISBN: 978-1-7391181-9-8

Contents

Preface — VII
The Magic of Mindsets
   Impact of Different Mindsets

1. Introduction to the World of Mindsets — 1
    What Is a Growth Mindset?
    The Power of Believing in Yourself
    Exploring the Differences: Fixed vs. Growth Mindsets

2. Unleashing Your Potential — 9
    Setting Exciting Goals with a Growth Mindset
    The Art of Positive Self-Talk
    Overcoming Limiting Beliefs

3. Embracing Challenges and Growing Stronger — 19
    Challenges Are Opportunities in Disguise
    Stepping Out of Your Comfort Zone
    Developing Resilience and Bouncing Back

4. Persistence — 29
    The Magic of Trying and Trying Again
    Learning from Mistakes and Failures
    Persevering Through Tough Times

5. Turning Setbacks into Comebacks — 37
    The Journey of the Fearless Athlete
    The Triumph of the Pop Sensation

    The Unstoppable Rise of the Magical Film Star

6. Perspective and Perception   47
   The Lens of Perception
   The Power of Positive Thinking
   Embracing Change with an Open Mind

7. Positive Self-Talk   55
   The Language of Positivity
   Taming the Inner Critic
   The Power of Affirmations

8. Affirmations   63
   When to Use Affirmations
   Affirmation Examples
   Situational Affirmations
   Lifelong Morning Affirmation
   Lifelong Nighttime Affirmation

9. The Power of YET   73
   I Can't Do It YET
   The Transformative Effect of Yet
   Embracing the Journey of Learning

10. The Secret Ingredient   81
    An Extraordinary Story
    Making Practice Fun and Effective
    Embracing Challenges as Exciting Adventures

11. Creating a Growth Mindset Environment   89
    Encouraging Supportive Friendships
    Nurturing a Growth Mindset at Home
    Building a Growth Mindset Classroom

12. The Magic of Failure and Feedback   101
    The Truth about Failure

       Real People Who Turned Failure into Success
       Embracing Feedback for Growth
       Learning to Improve through Feedback

13. Growth Mindset Superpowers   111
       Courage and Confidence
       Creativity and Innovation
       Empathy and Resilience

14. Continuing Your Mindset Magic Adventure   123
       Spreading Magic to Others
       Embracing a Lifetime of Growth
       You Are the Master of Your Mindset Journey

Conclusion   133

Which Door Will You Open?   137

Glossary   143

Preface

The Magic of Mindsets

First Scenario

Caroline loved to paint and spent hours creating colorful works of art in her room. One day, her friend Alex came over to watch her paint. Excited to start a new painting, she set up a blank canvas on her easel and began to work. However, as Caroline tried to bring her imagination to life, she encountered a challenging scene. Frustration overwhelmed her, and she started to believe painting this scene was too difficult.

Alex noticed Caroline's demeanor begin to change and began to worry about her. He thought that maybe she needed a break, so he decided to go downstairs and make them both a snack. Sharing a bite to eat and something to drink would give them the opportunity to chat.

While he was gone, Caroline began feeling defeated and discouraged. She put down her paintbrush and walked away from her unfinished work. Doubts filled her mind, and she started to question her artistic talent.

When he returned with the snacks, Alex noticed Caroline wasn't painting but sitting by the window, looking a little stressed, gazing at the canvas she had abandoned. He sensed her disappointment and wanted to encourage her to try again.

Caroline appreciated Alex's support but was still determining if she could overcome the obstacle.

After some time, Caroline was drawn back to her unfinished canvas. With determination in her eyes, she picked up her paintbrush once more. Caroline embraced the process, trying new brushstrokes and experimenting fearlessly. At one point, she thought she was making progress, as each stroke was a step closer to capturing the scene she envisioned.

However, as she persisted, Caroline's frustration grew stronger as she was not creating the desired effect. She began to believe her artistic talent was limited and would never improve. Finally, feeling totally disheartened, she abandoned the canvas again, convinced she wasn't cut out to be the great artist she had hoped to be.

As Caroline clung to the belief that her artistic abilities were fixed and unchangeable, her once vibrant passion for art began to fade. From that day forward, Caroline struggled to find the motivation to paint, and consequently, her dream of becoming a serious artist would never be reached.

Second Scenario

Wendy was passionate about playing the piano and spent hours practicing melodies that brought joy to the hearts of those who listened.

One day, she came across a challenging piece of music in her piano book. It was filled with complex notes and tricky rhythms that seemed almost impossible to master. Instead of feeling discouraged, her eyes lit up with excitement. She saw this as an opportunity to learn, grow, and improve her skills as a pianist.

With determination, Wendy placed her hands on the piano keys and started to play. The notes could have been better, and she stumbled on the tricky parts but kept going. She reminded herself that making mistakes was part of the learning process.

Each day, Wendy dedicated time to practicing the challenging piece. She focused on the parts that gave her trouble, working diligently to improve her abilities. Even when it felt frustrating, she kept going, knowing that effort and perseverance were the keys to progress.

Wendy's friend Amelia, an accomplished pianist herself, praised her dedication. "You're doing great, Wendy! Keep going, and you'll get better with each practice."

Wendy smiled and appreciated Amelia's support. She understood that improvement would not happen overnight and was excited about the journey ahead.

As the days turned into weeks, Wendy noticed significant progress. The tricky rhythms became more natural as her fingers danced gracefully across the keys. She felt a sense of achievement and knew that her growth mindset had led her to this success.

Wendy also understood that her journey as a pianist was only beginning. She continued to explore new pieces and challenges, each time embracing the opportunity to learn and grow.

With a growth mindset guiding her, Wendy knew there was no limit to what she could achieve, and with every note she played, she celebrated the joy of continuous improvement and the endless possibilities of her growth mindset.

Impact of Different Mindsets

These two stories showcase the profound impact of different mindsets on individuals' lives and achievements. In the first story, Caroline's fixed mindset hindered her ability to overcome challenges and pursue her passion for painting. Believing that her artistic talent was limited, Caroline felt defeated and discouraged when faced with difficulties.

This fixed mindset acted as a barrier, preventing her from embracing the opportunity to learn and grow as an artist. Ultimately, Caroline's fixed mindset led her to abandon her artistic pursuits, leaving her feeling unfulfilled and disconnected from her passion.

On the other hand, Wendy's growth mindset transformed her journey as a pianist. When confronted with a challenging piece of music, Wendy embraced it enthusiastically, seeing it as a chance to improve and develop her skills. With determination and a belief in her ability to learn and progress, she persevered through the difficulties of the piece.

Her growth mindset allowed her to view mistakes as part of the learning process, and she continued to practice diligently, celebrating her progress along the way. As a result, Wendy's growth mindset propelled her forward, leading her to achieve significant improvement and success in her piano playing.

These stories highlight our mindset's pivotal role in shaping our experiences and outcomes. A fixed mindset can lead to self-doubt, fear of failure, and a limited willingness to embrace challenges. This mindset often hinders personal growth and inhibits individuals from reaching their full potential.

Although Caroline and Wendy both faced challenges in their respective passions, their mindsets determined the trajectory of their journeys. In our own lives, the attitude we adopt can shape our passions, academic achievements, personal relationships, and career growth.

So, ask yourself, do you want to be more like Caroline or Wendy?

Embracing a growth mindset opens the doors to a more fulfilling and successful life, where we welcome new possibilities and experience the enchanting magic of continuous improvement.

If you want to be more like Wendy, then turn the page to *Introduction to the World of Mindsets*.

> "The only limit to our realization of tomorrow
> will be our doubts of today."
> - Franklin D. Roosevelt

Chapter 1

Introduction to the World of Mindsets

As a kid, I didn't fully grasp the significance of a growth mindset, and at that time I had never even heard of the concept. I often faced challenges, and instead of viewing them as opportunities to learn and grow, I would get discouraged quickly. The fear of failure and the thought of not being good enough haunted my young mind, causing me to give up too easily on tasks that didn't come naturally to me.

I vividly remember moments when I would receive constructive feedback or criticism from teachers, parents, or even friends. Instead of seeing it as a chance to improve, I would take it personally and get upset if I was told something I didn't want to hear. The idea of receiving feedback made me feel scared, and I struggled to understand that it was meant to help me grow rather than tear me down.

As a result, I would spend unnecessary time feeling miserable and sorry for myself, questioning my abilities. I should have recognized the value of perseverance and resilience when facing setbacks. Still, in those days, I didn't have the tools to cope with failure constructively, which hindered my progress in various aspects of my life.

It wasn't until I got older that I began to understand the importance of a growth mindset. Learning about the power of believing in myself and my ability to improve and to view challenges as stepping stones rather than obstacles was transformative. I discovered that embracing a growth mindset was not about avoiding failure but accepting it as a natural part of the learning process.

Once I embraced a growth mindset, I started to see the magic of feedback. Instead of feeling rejected, I began to welcome constructive criticism as valuable guidance for my growth. I learned to use feedback as a tool to refine my skills and make progress in various areas of my life.

I realized that giving up on challenges would never lead to growth and achievement. Learning to have a growth mindset allowed me to develop the persistence and determination to tackle complex tasks, even when they seemed impossible. With this new perspective, I felt empowered to face challenges head-on and invest time and effort to succeed.

As I continued to nurture my growth mindset, I became more resilient in the face of failure. I understood that setbacks were not indications of my worth but opportunities for improvement. Each failure became a valuable lesson, guiding me toward better strategies and a deeper understanding of my capabilities.

Looking back on my journey, I am grateful for the transformation that a growth mindset brought to my life. It has taught me to approach every situation with curiosity, determination, and a belief in my capacity to learn and adapt. I now understand that growth is a lifelong adventure. With a growth mindset as my compass, I am continually evolving and reaching new heights.

If I could go back in time, I would tell my younger self that the magic of a growth mindset lies in embracing challenges and seeing failures not as dead-ends but as stepping stones to success. It is the key to unlocking our true potential and living a life filled with possibilities and fulfillment. By cultivating a growth mindset from an early age, we empower ourselves to become the architects of our destiny and embark on a lifelong journey of growth, learning, and magical achievements.

But this doesn't have to be you! You don't need to go back in time. You are still your younger self and have the opportunity to get a head start in your life right now.

Welcome to **Mindset Magic: Growth Mindset for Kids**!

My name is Matthew Black, and I will guide your mindset magic journey.

Together, we will explore the importance of a growth mindset and positive self-talk for a happier and more purposeful life.

I know for many of you, this may be the first text-heavy non-fiction book you are reading. And that's a good thing – it's all part of your growth. You don't have to read it quickly or all in one go.

Take your time and re-read sections if you struggle the first time. I promise it will get easier as you make your way through the book.

Reading this book is the perfect example of rising to a challenge for your own self-improvement, and I'm really proud of you for doing so!

At the back of the book is a *Glossary*. This contains a list of words you may read in the book that you do not understand. If the word is there, you can find out exactly what it means.

Before the *Glossary*, you can use everything you learn in this book in a fun exercise by choosing the door you want to open as you face ten hypothetical situations.

Some points in the book are intentionally discussed more than once. You mustn't assume you already know everything because although the information might sound similar to what you've read before, there may be a twist, or it is explained in a different context.

By the end of this book, you will have all the knowledge and tools to guide you on your mindset magic journey to ensure you know how to develop a growth mindset and benefit from positive self-talk. This crucial life skill will empower you to navigate various situations confidently and successfully throughout your life.

In this chapter, we'll explore the magic of beliefs and how they shape how we learn and grow. Get ready to unlock the secrets of two extraordinary mindsets – the **fixed** and the **growth** mindsets.

You will learn to understand how these mindsets can influence your abilities, your confidence, and the way you face challenges. So, let's delve into the empowering world of a growth mindset, where effort, practice, and self-belief are the keys to reaching new heights. Let's embark on an enlightening voyage of self-discovery and transformation, where your mindset journey is as magical as the stars in the night sky!

What Is a Growth Mindset?

Imagine your brain is like a superhero's power. It's like having your very own magic wand inside your head! And do you know what this magical power is called? It's called a growth mindset – a unique way of thinking that helps you become even smarter and stronger!

With a growth mindset, you believe you can improve with effort and practice. It's like being on a thrilling adventure, facing challenges, and learning new things. Imagine you have a treasure map with all the knowledge and skills you want to discover, and every time you try something new, you take a step closer to uncovering those hidden treasures.

When you encounter tricky puzzles, complicated math problems, or even things you've never done, you feel excited instead of worried! You know that these challenges are opportunities for you to grow and learn. You use your brain and work hard to overcome these challenges like an apprentice magician training to become even more powerful.

And guess what? It's okay to make mistakes! Mistakes are like clues on your treasure map. Each time you make a mistake, you learn something new, guiding you to find the right path. So, don't be afraid of making mistakes because they are your superpower to become even better!

Sometimes, some people think their abilities are fixed, so they can't improve. That's called a fixed mindset. They might feel scared to try new things because they worry about failing or not being perfect, so they don't even try.

This doesn't have to be you!

With the magic of a growth mindset, you can improve and learn anything you put your mind to. Knowing you can handle challenges with your magical power, you can bravely face them.

You understand that effort and practice are like the secret spells that unlock your true potential!

So, always remember that you have the incredible power of a growth mindset inside you. Embrace challenges, believe in yourself, and keep practicing. You'll see how your magical power can make you shine and achieve amazing things!

When you keep growing and believing in yourself, you'll unlock the wonders of your limitless potential!

The Power of Believing in Yourself

Believing in yourself is a powerful and magical feeling. It means confidence in your abilities to do great things. Like a superhero with extraordinary power, believing in yourself gives you the same strength and courage to face challenges.

It's like having a secret power that boosts your confidence and helps you shine. You can use this magic to face challenges, make new friends, and achieve things you never thought possible.

Feeling a little nervous sometimes is okay, but when you believe in yourself, you can overcome those feelings and keep going. The power of self-belief empowers you to reach for your dreams and never give up, no matter how hard things may seem.

Everyone makes mistakes, but when you believe in yourself, you learn from them and use them to improve. You are your best friend, so be kind to yourself, celebrate your successes, and know that you can do amazing things.

With the power of believing in yourself, you're on an adventure of growth and learning, becoming the best version of yourself each day!

And you want to be the best version of yourself, right?

So, remember the incredible magic of believing in yourself. It's your key to unlocking all the exciting, extraordinary adventures and achievements in this incredible, magical world!

Keep believing, and you'll see how amazing you truly are!

Exploring the Differences: Fixed vs. Growth Mindsets

There are two ways of thinking – the fixed and the growth mindsets. Learning what they mean is essential to decide which mindset to adopt.

Fixed Mindset:

- Believes that abilities, talents, and intelligence are fixed and cannot be changed.

- Feels stuck and afraid to try new things, fearing failure or not being good enough.

- Views challenges as obstacles and may give up easily when faced with difficulties.

- Making mistakes is seen as a sign of not being smart.

- Thinks that effort and hard work may not lead to improvement since abilities are fixed.

- Doubt themselves and lack confidence in their abilities.

Growth Mindset:

- Believes that effort and practice can improve abilities, talents, and intelligence.

- Views challenges as opportunities to learn and develop, seeing them as exciting experiences.

- Persists through difficulties and sees setbacks as part of the learning process.

- Views mistakes as valuable lessons that guide learning for improvement.

- Understands that effort and hard work are essential for growth and development.

- Believes in themselves and their potential, using self-belief as a source of strength and confidence.

As you can see, a growth mindset opens possibilities and empowers you to achieve amazing things. By embracing a magical growth mindset, you can overcome challenges, learn new skills, and become the best version of yourself!

I'm sure you want to be the best version of yourself.

As you turn the page to the next chapter, *Unleashing Your Potential*, know you can create a life filled with courage, confidence, and boundless growth.

Trust in your abilities, believe in the magic of growth, and let your journey of self-discovery unfold like an extraordinary tale of bravery and triumph, for the world of endless possibilities awaits you!

Always remember, **you have the power** to choose your mindset! Keep growing, learning, and believing, and you'll soon see how wonderful and capable you are!

"Whether you think you can, or you think you can't – you're right."
- Henry Ford

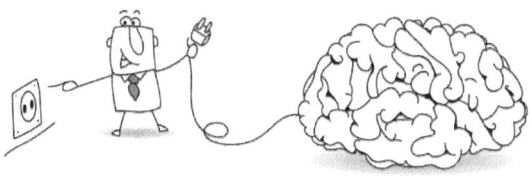

Chapter 2

Unleashing Your Potential

Let's unleash your limitless potential to become the best version of yourself!. Through the magic of a growth mindset, you'll learn how to tap into your abilities and talents, face challenges with courage, and achieve your dreams.

Setting Exciting Goals with a Growth Mindset

Setting goals means deciding on things you want to achieve or accomplish in the future. Goals can be about anything you choose. Getting into the habit of setting goals and working towards them at a young age will benefit you later in life.

Below are some goal-setting tips to help you get started:

Dream Big

Imagine having dreams as big as the sky – like becoming a scientist, a respected artist, or a sports champion! With a growth mindset, you know no goal is unreachable. As they say, aim for the moon, and if you miss, you'll land among the stars. Let your imagination soar, and always dream big!

Break It Down

Setting big goals can feel overwhelming, but don't worry! Break them into smaller steps, like a brave adventurer mapping out a quest. Each step becomes a thrilling mini-adventure, guiding you closer to your ultimate treasure.

Be Specific

Instead of saying, "I want to be better at math," be specific about your goal. For example, "I want to improve my multiplication skills by practicing daily." Specific goals help you focus and track your progress.

Plan and Practice

Setting goals is just the beginning. Create a plan to reach your goals, and practice regularly, just like a hero training for a grand challenge. The more you practice, the better you will become and the closer you will be to achieving your dreams. Don't get lazy or complacent, and always stick to your plan!

Embrace Challenges

Challenges may come your way as you work towards your goals. Never let obstacles or challenges deter you. Embrace these challenges with courage and determination. See them as opportunities to learn and grow stronger. Don't let fear stop you from achieving your dreams. The greatest rewards are often found after demanding challenges and obstacles.

Celebrate Progress

Even if you still need to reach your goal, celebrate your progress! Every forward step you take is a step closer to your dreams.

Being constant and brave, even by taking baby steps, will yield you results. With each step you achieve, your confidence will increase, and as your confidence increases, so will your ability to reach your goals.

Stay Positive

Sometimes, things may go differently than planned, but never lose heart! With a growth mindset, you understand that success takes time and effort. Stay positive and keep believing in yourself. Learn to see the glass half full as opposed to half empty.

Adjust and Keep Going

Goals may change as you grow and discover new interests. Be flexible and adjust your plans accordingly. Remember, setting and achieving goals is ongoing, and there's always something exciting to find.

> *With a growth mindset, you have a magical compass that guides you to the stars. Embrace the enchanting adventure of setting exciting goals, and let the journey of self-belief and achievement unfold. Believe in yourself, dream big, and let your growth mindset lead you to endless possibilities!*

The Art of Positive Self-Talk

Positive self-talk is a powerful tool that boosts your confidence, brightens your spirit, and leads you to greater success. Imagine having a special friend inside your head, always cheering you on and encouraging you every step of the way.

I can't express the importance of the words you tell yourself. Over time, you will begin to believe those words and act in accordance with those beliefs. How you look at things will determine any outcomes. With positive self-talk, you become your biggest supporter, as the magic lies in how you talk to yourself.

The art of positive self-talk is a magical key that unlocks your true potential. Like a wizard's wand casting spells, your thoughts and beliefs shape your actions and decisions.

When you practice positive self-talk, you fill your mind with empowering thoughts, boosting your confidence and banishing self-doubt.

This magical practice improves your self-esteem and helps you navigate challenges with resilience and determination. You create a powerful foundation for personal growth and success by cultivating a growth mindset through positive self-talk.

Remember, how you talk to yourself matters. Learn to catch negative thoughts immediately and make a deliberate effort to change them before they take root and amplify, affecting all areas of your life.

> *Self-talk can either hold you back or propel you on the exciting journey of becoming the best version of yourself. Focus on the art of positive self-talk, and watch as it weaves its magic, guiding you toward a brighter and more fulfilling future!*

So, how exactly do you do this?

Be Your Best Friend

Treat yourself like a kind and caring friend.

When you face challenges or setbacks, talk to yourself with the same love, understanding, and encouragement you would offer a needy friend. Replace self-criticism with self-compassion and watch your confidence soar.

Banish Negative Thoughts

Negative thoughts can feel like dark clouds casting shadows on your dreams. Learn to spot them and challenge their validity. Replace negative thoughts with positive and uplifting affirmations, like "I can do this!" or "I am capable and strong!"

Celebrate Your Strengths

Acknowledge and celebrate your strengths, commitment, and achievements like a painter admiring their masterpiece. When you complete a challenging task or achieve a goal, pat yourself on the back and say, "I did it!" This should be celebrated because you didn't give up, even if it would have been the easier thing to do at the time!

Embrace Mistakes as Learning Opportunities

Mistakes are stepping stones to success, not signs of failure. When you make a mistake, don't be too hard on yourself. Instead, see it as a chance to learn and grow. Say, "It's okay to make mistakes; I can learn from them and do better next time." You can also not take yourself too seriously and laugh and say something like, "Well, I won't be doing it like that again!"

Reframe Challenges

Instead of seeing challenges as roadblocks, view them as exciting puzzles or adventures to conquer. When faced with a difficult task, say, "I love challenges because they make me stronger and smarter!" or even something as simple as "I've got this!"

Focus on Effort

Sometimes, success takes time and effort. Rather than just focusing on the outcome, celebrate the effort you put into something. Say, "I'm proud of how hard I worked, and I'll keep improving."

Surround Yourself with Positivity

Just like a garden needs sunshine and water to thrive, you must surround yourself with positive people who uplift and inspire you. Listen to motivational podcasts or read books that encourage a growth mindset.

Practice, Practice, Practice

Positive self-talk takes practice, like learning a new spell. Be patient with yourself, and keep practicing. The more you do it, the stronger and more natural it will become.

> *Remember, you can transform your feelings with positive self-talk. By believing in yourself, encouraging your efforts, and embracing challenges, you unleash the magic of a growth mindset and pave the way for a more confident and blooming you.*

So, let the art of positive self-talk always be your guiding star as you journey through the wonderful world of self-discovery and growth.

Overcoming Limiting Beliefs

Limiting beliefs can be like heavy chains that hold you back from living a fulfilling and joyful life. These beliefs become self-fulfilling prophecies when you believe you can't do something or are not good enough. They create a fixed mindset that stifles your potential and prevents you from taking risks or exploring new opportunities.

When you believe you can't do something, you won't be able to do it. As a result, you may miss out on exciting adventures and valuable learning experiences that could lead to personal growth and success.

Limiting beliefs can impact your self-esteem and confidence negatively. When you constantly tell yourself that you're not capable or worthy, it takes a toll on your self-image. You may start to doubt yourself and become hesitant to try new things or take on challenges.

This lack of self-belief can hinder your progress and prevent you from achieving your goals.

Limiting beliefs leads to a fear of failure, which can be paralyzing. When you believe failure is something to be avoided at all costs, you may avoid taking risks or trying new things.

This fear of failure can trap you in your comfort zone, preventing you from exploring your full potential and discovering new talents and abilities.

Additionally, limiting beliefs can negatively impact your relationships with others. When you doubt yourself or feel unworthy, this affects how you interact with friends, family, and teachers. You may hold back from sharing your ideas or expressing yourself, fearing judgment or rejection. This can lead to missing opportunities and connections with others.

Overcoming limiting beliefs is crucial for your personal growth and well-being. When you replace limiting beliefs with empowering ones, you open yourself to a world of possibilities. Embracing a growth mindset allows you to view challenges as opportunities for learning and growth. It empowers you to take on new challenges with confidence and resilience, knowing you can learn and improve.

Shedding the weight of limiting beliefs allows you to pursue your passions and dreams wholeheartedly. You see setbacks as stepping stones to success and embrace failures as valuable lessons. With a positive and empowering mindset, you'll cultivate self-belief, build your self-esteem, and develop the courage to pursue your goals and aspirations.

There are times when limiting beliefs may cast shadows on your journey. These beliefs are like invisible barriers that hold you back from reaching your true potential. With the power of a growth mindset, you can overcome these limiting beliefs and set yourself free.

Identify Your Limiting Beliefs

Recognizing them is the first step in overcoming limiting beliefs. Pay attention to thoughts that start with "I can't," "I'm not good enough," or "I'll never be able to." These are clues that you have limiting beliefs that need to be challenged.

Question Their Validity

Question the evidence behind your limiting beliefs like a detective solving a mystery. Ask yourself, "Is this belief true?" or "What proof do I have that this is accurate?" Often, you'll find that these beliefs are based on assumptions rather than facts.

Replace with Empowering Beliefs

Once you've identified and questioned your limiting beliefs, replace them with empowering ones that support your growth and potential. For example, turn "I can't do it" into "I can learn and improve with effort."

Challenge Your Comfort Zone

Limiting beliefs thrive in comfort zones, like weeds in a garden. It's called a comfort zone because that's where you are the most comfortable. Unfortunately, this is not where you will grow and develop.

You need to make an effort to step outside the safety of your comfort zone to reach your full potential by trying new things. As you do, you'll discover that your abilities are more expansive than you once believed. We will discuss this in more detail in the next chapter.

Embrace Failures as Lessons

Instead of fearing failure, see it as part of your journey to success. See mistakes as valuable lessons that guide your growth. Remember, failure is a part of the journey, and every setback brings you closer to reaching your potential.

Seek Support and Encouragement

Like a team of allies supporting a hero, surround yourself with people who uplift and encourage you. Share your journey with friends, family, or mentors who believe in your potential and provide guidance.

Practice Self-Compassion

Everyone faces challenges and doubts, so remember to be kind to yourself. Treat yourself with the same care, understanding, and compassion you would offer a needy friend.

Visualize Your Success

Imagine yourself overcoming challenges and achieving your goals confidently. Visualization can be a powerful tool in rewiring your beliefs and boosting your self-belief.

Close your eyes and create images in your mind of the outcome you want. Focus on how this makes you feel, and then carry that feeling with you on your journey.

Overcoming limiting beliefs is like unlocking the door to your true potential. Don't let these beliefs stop you from becoming the best version of yourself!

> *By challenging negative thoughts, embracing growth, and positively surrounding yourself, you'll break free from the chains of limiting beliefs and soar to new heights. With the magic of a growth mindset guiding you, you'll embark on an extraordinary journey of self-discovery, where the possibilities are as vast and boundless as the stars in the night sky.*

Always **believe in yourself**, for the adventure of overcoming limiting beliefs leads to a world of endless opportunities and limitless potential!

Let's discover more about *Embracing Challenges and Growing Stronger*.

> *"Shoot for the moon.*
> *Even if you miss, you'll land among the stars."*
> \- Norman Vincent Peale

Chapter 3

Embracing Challenges and Growing Stronger

You are now about to discover that challenges are opportunities for growth and self-discovery. Let the magic of your growth mindset guide you as you explore the power of stepping out of your comfort zone to face difficulties with bravery so you can become resilient and bounce back even stronger.

Challenges Are Opportunities in Disguise

In the world of a growth mindset, challenges are like thrilling adventures that lead you to hidden treasures of growth. At first, challenges might seem tough, like tricky riddles or puzzling quests, but don't worry – they are magical opportunities in disguise!

Imagine you're a brave hero where each challenge is like a secret door to new possibilities. With a growth mindset, you know that challenges are not scary monsters but stepping stones toward becoming even stronger and smarter.

So, how can you embrace challenges and turn them into exciting opportunities?

Stay Curious

Instead of being afraid, be curious about the challenge ahead. Ask questions and be eager to learn as you face the unknown. The more you know, the more familiar you will be and the less anxious you will feel.

See Mistakes as Stepping Stones

Mistakes are like magical clues that guide you forward. Don't fear them, but rather learn from them and use them to move closer to your goals.

Believe In Your Magic

Trust your abilities and know you can conquer challenges with effort and practice. Believe in the magic of your growth mindset.

Break It Down

Just like a challenging puzzle, break big challenges into smaller pieces. Take one step at a time and celebrate your progress along the way. It's much easier to complete a more minor task or a few smaller challenges than one big one, especially if it is something new to you.

Seek Help from Allies

Be bold and ask for help. Heroes have allies, and seeking support from friends, family, or teachers can make the journey more accessible and fun. Getting support from other people who have experience is always beneficial.

Stay Positive

Keep a positive attitude, and tap into your inner light like sunshine on a cloudy day. Replace "I can't do it" with "I can learn and improve with each try!" The more you learn and try, the more you will feel your confidence growing and see the benefits of staying positive.

Celebrate Each Victory

Every little victory is a triumph in itself. Celebrate your efforts and progress, and know you are growing stronger with every challenge you face.

> *With your growth mindset as your magical guide, you can transform challenges into thrilling adventures of self-discovery and growth. Embrace challenges with courage, curiosity, and the belief that you can do amazing things. The journey of a growth mindset awaits you, filled with endless opportunities and the enchanting magic of becoming the best version of yourself!*

Stepping Out of Your Comfort Zone

As previously mentioned, there's a place called the comfort zone. It's like a cozy castle where you feel safe and familiar. But here's the secret: The real magic happens when you are brave and step out of your comfort zone to embark on daring adventures!

Stepping out of your comfort zone is trying things you haven't tried before, like being a brave adventurer exploring uncharted lands. It might feel a little scary at first, but that's okay! It's like trying a new spell – you won't know how powerful it is until you try it.

So many people are afraid to step out of their comfort zones and miss out on many experiences life has to offer because of this fear. Don't let this be you!

Imagine if you had been too reluctant to try your favorite food for the first time because it was unfamiliar. I bet you're glad you did!

Stepping out of your comfort zone doesn't mean doing something reckless or harmful, but rather doing something that most people do that you personally might find a little scary.

> *I also want you to know that you don't have to do everything others do. You have nothing to prove, and if you don't want to do something, that's okay. Just make sure you do or don't do something for the right reasons.*

I remember going to a fair where a man had a python that you could hold. Many of my friends decided to go and pick up the snake, but not me. I couldn't even bear to watch. This was one instance where I was more than comfortable staying in my comfort zone, and that was perfectly okay.

This may sound contradictory, but as long as you come out of your comfort zone at other times, this is perfectly acceptable.

What can you do to get out of your comfort zone and unlock new magic levels in your life?

Embrace New Experiences

Like discovering a hidden treasure, be open to trying things you've never done before. It could be joining a new club, learning a new skill, or making new friends. It's so important when you're young to embrace new experiences, as it's only through experience that you begin to know what you really enjoy and what you want in life.

Face Small Fears

Every hero faces fears, but they also find the courage to overcome them. Start by facing small fears, like speaking up in class or trying a new sport. Each little step helps you grow bolder. If it doesn't go well the first time, don't give up because I promise it will get easier over time.

Take On Challenges

Challenges outside your comfort zone are like thrilling quests that lead to growth. Whether tackling a tricky math problem or presenting something to your class, believe in yourself and take the leap!

Learn from Setbacks

Even the bravest adventurers face setbacks, but they never give up. When things don't go as planned, see it as a chance to learn and improve, like a brave knight learning from battles.

Ask for Help

Heroes rely on their allies, and you have them too! If you feel overwhelmed when stepping out of your comfort zone, don't hesitate to seek support from trusted friends, family, or teachers.

Celebrate Your Bravery

Celebrate your bravery each time you step out of your comfort zone! Even if things don't go perfectly, know you're growing stronger and more resilient with every adventure. The fact that you stepped out of your comfort zone is a cause for celebration in itself, so don't ever underestimate that.

Stepping out of your comfort zone is like discovering hidden chambers of courage and confidence within yourself. It's the path to unlocking new magical abilities and reaching for the stars.

Embrace the magic of your growth mindset, and let it guide you as you step boldly into new territories of self-discovery and personal growth. The adventure of stepping out of your comfort zone awaits, and with it comes the incredible magic of becoming the fearless hero of your own story!

Developing Resilience and Bouncing Back

Resilience is like a powerful shield that helps you bounce back from tough times. Life is like a roller coaster ride, with many ups and downs, but with resilience, you can face challenges like a brave hero!

Resilience is the magical ability to stay strong and positive when things get tough. It's like having a secret potion that helps you keep going, no matter what. This is something you can tap into whenever you need it.

So, how can you develop resilience and become a resilient hero?

Believe In Yourself

Trust your abilities and know you have the strength to overcome difficulties. Believe that you can handle anything that comes your way. The more you succeed, the stronger your belief in yourself will become, enabling you to take on more significant challenges.

Stay Positive

Always focus on having a positive attitude, especially in tough times, like a little spark that lights up the dark. Focus on the good things and use challenges as opportunities to grow. Although it is not always easy to keep positive, if you can master this ability from a young age, it will help shape your life positively.

Learn from Setbacks

Every brave adventurer faces setbacks, but they don't let them stop their journey. When things don't go as planned, see it as another chance to learn and grow stronger and use that experience to improve next time.

You will discover more about this in the chapter, *Turning Setbacks into Comebacks*.

Practice Problem-Solving

Resilience is like being a clever puzzle solver. When faced with difficulties, think of creative ways to solve the problem and find a way forward.

Take Care of Yourself

Just like heroes, rest and recharge and take care of yourself. Sleep well, eat healthy foods, keep hydrated, and take breaks as needed. Self-care should become an integral part of your lifestyle.

Keep a Growth Mindset

Remember that challenges are part of the journey. Keep a growth mindset and believe you can learn and improve, even from the most challenging experiences.

Believe In Your Strength

Resilience begins with believing in your inner strength. Know you can overcome difficulties, just like a brave hero defeating villains.

Maintain a Positive Attitude

A positive attitude is like a shield that guards you from negativity. There is always something to learn and improve from challenges, and with a positive attitude, you'll find the silver lining in every cloud.

Accept Imperfections

Heroes are not flawless, and that's okay! You don't have to be perfect. You are a unique individual with your own personality. Embrace your mistakes as part of your heroic journey. Remember, even your parents and teachers sometimes make mistakes.

Seek Support

Like allies supporting a hero, lean on friends, family, or teachers when times get tough. Their encouragement and guidance can be like magical potions that heal and strengthen you. So always seek support and advice from people you trust.

Setbacks Are Stepping Stones

Instead of seeing setbacks as dead ends, view them as stepping stones to success. Each time you fall, you learn, grow, and bounce back higher. Being able to learn from mistakes is crucial to your self-development. With each setback, you have the opportunity to become better and better.

Practice Self-Compassion

Be kind to yourself like a gentle healer treating a wounded hero. Treat yourself with the same compassion you would offer a friend facing challenges.

Keep Moving Forward

Resilience is not about never falling but about getting up each time you do. Keep moving forward, and know that each step builds your strength and leads you to victory.

Developing resilience is like forging a powerful armor that protects you in the face of difficulties. It helps you stand tall when things get rough and gives you the courage to keep moving forward.

Embrace the magic of resilience, and let it guide you as you face challenges with bravery and determination. The adventure of developing resilience awaits, and with it comes the incredible magic of becoming an unwavering hero in the story of your life!

Rise to the challenges that await, for they are stepping stones toward greatness. Keep your growth mindset as your guide, and know that you have the power to create a future filled with endless possibilities. Your journey of self-discovery continues, and the promise of an extraordinary and courageous adventure comes with it.

As you turn the page to the next chapter, *Persistence*, be prepared to unlock the magic of hard work, dedication, and determination. It is through these qualities that you will uncover the true wonders that lie within you.

> *"Believe you can and you're halfway there."*
> \- Theodore Roosevelt

Chapter 4

Persistence

In this chapter, you will discover the secret to unlocking the true power of hard work, dedication, and unwavering determination. You will learn that most success follows persistence. It's often easy to give up, and for those who do, their goals will always remain goals. However, for those who persist in achieving their goals, sooner or later, they will be successful.

The Magic of Trying and Trying Again

Once upon a time, a young apprentice named Gina lived in a land where magic and a growth mindset intertwined. She dreamed of becoming a skilled magician, but her spells often went awry, and her potions fizzled instead of sparkling. Disheartened, she approached her wise mentor, Master Sage, seeking guidance.

Master Sage smiled warmly and said, "*Ah, young Gina, remember that the journey of a magician is not always smooth. It's in the magic of trying and trying again where true mastery is found.*"

Gina's eyes widened in curiosity, eager to learn the secrets of this magic. Master Sage shared these valuable insights:

Embrace the Learning Process

Every try is a chance to learn and improve. Each attempt nurtures your skills and talents like a seed sprouts into a mighty tree.

Challenges Are Opportunities

Don't fear challenges. They are gateways to growth. Like a puzzle waiting to be solved, each challenge holds the potential to reveal your hidden abilities. The more pieces of yourself you find, the stronger and more capable you will become.

Resilience

Like a phoenix rising from ashes, resilience empowers you to bounce back from failures. It's the unwavering belief in yourself that fuels your journey forward.

Growth Mindset

Embrace the power of a growth mindset. Believe that your talents can be developed through dedication and hard work. With this mindset, obstacles become stepping stones to greatness.

Celebrate the Journey

Each milestone is a victory to be celebrated. Appreciate and acknowledge the progress you make on your magical journey. People often say it is not about the destination but about the journey. So, no matter what happens, enjoy your journey!

Inspired by Master Sage's wisdom, Gina began her quest with determination. She practiced tirelessly, embracing failures as stepping stones to success. Her spells grew stronger with each attempt, and her potions sparkled brilliantly.

As Gina continued her magical journey, she realized that the magic of trying and trying again was not just about achieving success but embracing the process. It was about growing, learning, and becoming the best version of herself.

Like Gina, let the magic of effort and persistence guide you. Embrace the challenges, celebrate your progress, and remember that the journey is key to your true potential.

> *As you enter the unknown, the magic of trying and trying again will light your way, leading you to a future of limitless growth and enchanting achievements.*

Learning from Mistakes and Failures

Mistakes and failures are not signs of defeat but opportunities for growth and learning. Like a skilled sorcerer refining their spells, the secret to unlocking this magic lies in embracing the valuable lessons that mistakes and failures offer.

Without making mistakes, you wouldn't have the opportunity to improve. Your skills and confidence would stay the same, making it impossible to reach your full potential. As you already have so many qualities within yourself, it would be a real shame not to uncover them.

Use the following steps to learn from your mistakes:

Embrace the Power of Reflection

Instead of shying away from mistakes, please take a moment to reflect on what went wrong and why it turned out the way it did.

Like a curious scholar studying ancient scrolls, seek insights and understanding from each experience.

Turn Failures into Feedback

See failures as feedback, not final judgments. Use this feedback to adjust your approach and improve your skills like a compass guiding you toward the right path.

Learn the Art of Perseverance

The growth journey is not always smooth, but like a brave adventurer, perseverance is your ally. Don't let setbacks discourage you. Always use them to fuel your determination to keep trying.

Embrace the Growth Mindset

When you have a growth mindset, you believe your abilities can be developed through consistent effort and practice. Embrace the idea that mistakes are part of the learning process and that you can improve with each try.

Celebrate Mistakes as Learning Opportunities

Like discovering a hidden treasure, celebrate mistakes as valuable learning opportunities. The more you learn, the more powerful and wise you become on your magical journey.

Practice Self-Compassion

As a gentle healer tends to wounds, be kind to yourself when mistakes occur. Treat yourself with compassion and understanding, knowing that mistakes are natural steps on the path of growth.

Embrace a "Yet" Mentality

Replace "I can't do it" with "I can't do it yet." Like a patient gardener nurturing a seed, recognize that growth takes time and effort.

Believe in your potential to learn and improve over time. We will discuss this in more detail in a later chapter.

> *Learning from mistakes and failures unlocks the hidden gems of growth and understanding. Remember, the true magic of a growth mindset lies in your ability to see setbacks as stepping stones toward greatness.*

Embrace the power of learning from mistakes and failures. Let it guide you toward becoming an even more accomplished and resilient adventurer on your self-discovery and magical growth path.

Persevering Through Tough Times

Perseverance is a powerful ability that helps you navigate the darkest challenges. Like a courageous knight facing formidable foes, the secret to unlocking this magic lies in your unwavering determination and resilience during tough times.

Believe In Your Inner Strength

Perseverance starts with believing in your inner strength. Like a mighty fortress, you have the power to endure and overcome adversity. If you persevere, you will become closer to achieving your goals.

Stay Focused On Your Goals

Just as a skilled archer stays focused on the target, keep your eyes on your goals during tough times. Let your vision guide you through the storm, and remember the magic that awaits beyond the clouds. Don't be tempted to lower your goal. Instead, take a step back, rethink, and come back ready to give it another go.

Trust the Journey

Perseverance is like a winding path through an enchanted forest. Trust that every step you take, even if uncertain, leads you closer to triumph. Sometimes, things happen for a reason, meaning something better awaits you further down your path, even if you can't see it yet.

Learn from Challenges

Tough times are not roadblocks but growth opportunities. Like a wise sage gaining wisdom from ancient times, seek to learn from challenges and use that knowledge to become even better and stronger.

Find Support in Allies

Like loyal companions on a quest, seek support from friends, family, or mentors during tough times. Their encouragement and guidance can be the spark that ignites your inner fire.

Cultivate Resilience

Resilience is the armor that protects you in battle. Strengthen your resilience through positive self-talk and the belief that you can overcome any obstacle that comes your way.

Keep Moving Forward

In facing adversity, keep moving forward like a river flowing steadily. Perseverance is not about speed but steadfastness on the journey.

Celebrate Your Courage

Just as a kingdom honors its brave defenders, celebrate your courage and determination during tough times. Always acknowledge your efforts and the progress you make.

With the magic of perseverance, you can weather any storm and emerge stronger than ever. Tough times are not barriers but stepping stones on your path of growth. Embrace the magic of perseverance, and let it be your guiding light through challenging moments. As you persist, remember that the hero's journey is not only about the destination but the transformative adventure of becoming the hero of your extraordinary tale.

Think of books you've read and movies you've watched where the hero in the story had to overcome a challenge. What did they do? Did they give up or persevere and overcome the challenge? Are stories not more interesting when the main character faces his fear and overcomes the difficulty, leading to an inspiring ending?

This is how you want to be in your own life story.

As you continue your journey, remember that perseverance is not just to be used in tough times but should be a lifelong ally in pursuing your dreams. With each step forward, you will grow stronger and more resilient, ready to face any challenges that come your way.

Let this chapter be a testament to the indomitable spirit within you, guiding you toward a future of boundless possibilities. As you turn the page to the next chapter, *Turning Setbacks into Comebacks*, know that your seeds of perseverance will blossom into extraordinary achievements.

*"Your mind is a powerful thing.
When you fill it with positive thoughts, your life will start to change."*
- Anonymous

Chapter 5

Turning Setbacks into Comebacks

Have you ever watched somebody do something so well that you felt mesmerized watching them? Whether it's watching two ice skaters creating magic on the ice or somebody delivering a speech that makes you wish you had that talent, too.

Do you think they were born with those abilities, or do you think they persisted in honing their skills and practicing over time? And even then, do you think it was always easy?

In this chapter, we will explore the transformative magic that unfolds when ordinary people overcome challenges and bounce back more vital than ever.

Life's journey is a rollercoaster ride, and setbacks are an inevitable part of the adventure. But with the power of a growth mindset, setbacks become the catalysts for extraordinary achievements.

Let's appreciate the inspiring stories of extraordinary individuals who have faced setbacks and emerged victorious. These are not fictional tales but true accounts of resilience, determination, and an unwavering belief in the magic of a growth mindset.

All these people are extraordinary because they put the "**extra**" into the ordinary with their growth mindsets and determination, positivity, resilience, and bravery.

As we explore the lives of these remarkable people, draw inspiration from their experiences. You will witness the profound transformation when setbacks are embraced as opportunities for growth and self-discovery.

So, learn from their journeys and understand the true essence of a growth mindset. Let the stories of these real people guide you, showing you how to embrace challenges so you can bounce back with newfound strength.

As you unlock the secrets of their success, may the magic of a growth mindset become an ever-present companion on your path to triumph and personal growth.

The Journey of the Fearless Athlete

A young girl named Serena Williams dreamed of being a tennis champion. From a very early age, Serena and her sister Venus were introduced to the exciting world of tennis by their father, Richard Williams. He saw the spark of talent within his daughters and decided to train them to become tennis stars.

As Serena grew older, her magical journey was challenging. She faced skepticism and doubts from some who questioned whether she could succeed due to her race and background. But Serena refused to be defined by others' expectations. With a growth mindset, she believed that overcoming any obstacle was possible.

Serena's determination to succeed was tested on the professional tennis circuit. She encountered setbacks and defeats but refused to let failure define her each time. Instead, she saw these moments as opportunities to learn and grow.

Through hard work, dedication, and an unwavering belief in her abilities, Serena transformed herself into a powerful force on the tennis court. Her game was filled with magic - incredible serves, lightning-fast footwork, and a competitive spirit that knew no bounds.

In 1999, at just 17 years old, Serena won her first Grand Slam singles title at the US Open, and her magic began shining even brighter. Over the years, she continued to dominate the tennis world, winning numerous Grand Slam titles, including:

Wimbledon Championships: Serena has won the prestigious Wimbledon title multiple times, showcasing her skill and finesse on the grass court with sheer determination.

Australian Open: Serena claimed victory in the Australian Open several times, displaying her relentless pursuit of excellence and ability to adapt to different playing conditions.

French Open: Known for her versatility, Serena also triumphed in the challenging clay courts of the French Open, proving her prowess on various surfaces.

US Open: Serena captivated audiences in her home Grand Slam with her incredible performances, demonstrating her ability to handle immense pressure gracefully.

Throughout her journey, Serena faced fierce opponents and personal challenges. She battled injuries and setbacks, but her growth mindset remained unshakeable. Each time she stumbled, she picked herself up, stronger and more determined than before.

Off the court, Serena became a symbol of empowerment and a role model for aspiring athletes, especially young girls of diverse backgrounds. She used her voice to advocate for gender equality and social justice, inspiring others to dream big and break barriers.

Serena Williams' story is a testament to the magic of a growth mindset. It taught her that failures are not roadblocks and that anything is possible with determination, hard work, and belief in oneself. She proved that a strong mind and relentless effort can lead to enchanted success.

> *Through Serena's journey, you can learn the power of resilience and the importance of staying true to your dreams, no matter the challenges. With a growth mindset, you, too, can transform setbacks into magical comebacks and write your own inspiring stories of triumph and greatness.*

In 2021, a movie called King Richard, starring Will Smith, showcased her incredible journey. If you would like to find out more about Serena's journey, it's well worth watching.

The Triumph of the Pop Sensation

Ariana Grande had a passion for singing and performing from a young age. With her enchanting voice and captivating stage presence, she dreamt of becoming a world-renowned pop sensation.

Ariana faced various challenges and obstacles as she started her musical journey. Initially, she auditioned for talent shows and competitions, but only some doors opened. Some people told her she wasn't the right fit or her voice needed improvement. Despite these setbacks, Ariana never lost her belief in herself and her music.

With a growth mindset, Ariana used each setback as an opportunity for growth and learning. She dedicated herself to vocal training and dance lessons, tirelessly honing her skills to become the best version of herself. Ariana knew that success wasn't immediate, but she was committed to the magic of hard work and perseverance.

Her breakthrough moment came when she auditioned for a singing competition on television. Although she didn't win the show, her mesmerizing voice caught the attention of music producers. They saw the potential in her and offered her a recording contract.

As a pop star, Ariana faced the pressure of fame, public scrutiny, and relentless schedules. But her growth mindset remained her anchor in the whirlwind of success. She embraced the challenges, continuously pushing herself to improve and evolve as an artist.

Ariana's magical voice and powerful performances soon captured the hearts of fans worldwide. With chart-topping hits and sold-out concerts, she soared to stardom. Yet, her journey wasn't without hardships.

In 2017, a tragic event shook the world when a terrorist attack occurred at one of her concerts. The incident left Ariana and her fans devastated. But instead of letting fear consume her, Ariana channeled her resilience and love into the healing power of music. She arranged a benefit concert to raise funds for the victims and families affected, showing the world the magic of compassion and unity.

Throughout her career, Ariana continued to evolve and experiment with her music. From pop anthems to soulful ballads, she fearlessly embraced change and growth. Her songs became empowering anthems of self-love, strength, and overcoming hardships.

Today, Ariana is a pop sensation celebrated for her enchanting vocals, fearless artistry, and unwavering authenticity. She uses her fame to advocate for mental health awareness and social causes, inspiring her fans to believe in themselves and embrace their uniqueness.

Ariana's story teaches us the importance of believing in our dreams, even when faced with setbacks. With a growth mindset, we can use challenges as stepping stones to magical success.

> Like Ariana, you can transform your setbacks into powerful comebacks and share your unique magic with the world. So, embrace your talents, face the challenges with determination, and let the power of a growth mindset guide you to extraordinary heights!

The Unstoppable Rise of the Magical Film Star

From a young age, Leonardo DiCaprio was drawn to the magic of storytelling and the art of acting. With a dream in his heart and a passion for acting, he set out on a magical journey to become one of the most acclaimed actors in the world.

Leonardo faced his share of challenges and setbacks along the way. Despite his talent and dedication early in his career, he struggled to land significant film roles. But Leonardo refused to let rejections dim his magical light. With a growth mindset, he embraced every experience as a chance to learn and grow as an actor.

His breakthrough came when he starred in the critically acclaimed movie "Titanic." The film's monumental success catapulted Leonardo to superstardom, and his magic lit up the silver screen. Audiences fell in love with his captivating performance, and he became a global household name.

Leonardo continued to take on diverse and challenging roles as his career blossomed. He delved deep into the character's emotions and experiences with each film, leaving audiences in awe of his talent. He fearlessly explored different genres and collaborated with renowned directors to create cinematic masterpieces.

Throughout his journey, Leonardo has demonstrated his dedication to his craft and to positively impacting the world. He used his influence to advocate for environmental causes and raise awareness about climate change. Leonardo believed in the power of his platform. He used it to inspire others to take action and protect our planet's magic.

Even with immense fame and success, Leonardo stayed grounded, humble, and committed to growth. He never stopped striving to perfect his artistry, attending acting workshops and seeking feedback to continue improving.

Today, Leonardo is celebrated as one of the most esteemed actors in the industry. He has received numerous accolades, including Academy Awards, for his captivating performances. Yet, his magical journey is far from over, as he continues to enchant us with his talent and dedication to his craft.

Leonardo's story teaches us the magic of believing in ourselves and persevering through challenges. We can transform setbacks into stepping stones to success with a growth mindset. Like Leonardo, we can embrace every opportunity to learn, improve, and shine brightly uniquely.

So, embrace your dreams, believe in your abilities, and let the power of a growth mindset guide you on your own magical journey to success.

> *With passion, dedication, and unwavering belief, you can create a story as enchanting as Leonardo DiCaprio's and make your mark in the world.*

In the enthralling world of entertainment and sport, you have witnessed the awe-inspiring journeys of real-life pop stars, film stars, and athletes who embraced the magic of a growth mindset. These remarkable individuals demonstrated the power of believing in oneself, persevering through challenges, and transforming setbacks into stepping stones to success.

From the enchanting rise of the pop sensation to the star-studded path of the resilient film star and the triumphant journey of the fearless athlete, one common thread unites them all - the growth mindset.

These exceptional individuals did not let rejections, doubts, or setbacks define their destinies. Instead, they used every experience as an opportunity to learn, improve, and grow.

Reflecting on their magical stories, realize that a growth mindset is a superpower that knows no limits. It empowers you to face challenges with courage, embrace change enthusiastically, and turn failures into fuel for progress.

As you journey through life, remember the magic of the growth mindset. Embrace your dreams, believe in your abilities, and let determination and perseverance light your path. When faced with setbacks, summon the courage to transform them into comebacks, and let the belief in your magic lead you to extraordinary heights.

Whether you dream of standing on the world's biggest stages as a pop star, gracing the silver screen like a film star, or conquering the arenas as a fearless athlete, remember that you hold the key to your own success.

With a growth mindset, you can create your enchanting story and make a lasting impact on the world.

Your journey is just beginning, and the possibilities are endless. The stars are waiting to witness your brilliance, and the world eagerly awaits you to be enchanted by the magic within you.

As you continue your magical adventure, never forget that you are the master of your mindset journey. You shape your destiny with every step you take and manifest your potential with every dream you chase.

So, go forth and unleash the power of your growth mindset, for **the world is yours to enchant**, and the magic of your potential is boundless.

The next chapter will teach you about *Perspective and Perception*, both valuable in progressing your journey.

"The only way to achieve the impossible is to believe it is possible."
- Charles Kingsleigh (Alice in Wonderland)

Chapter 6

Perspective and Perception

Perspectives are the unique lenses through which we perceive the world around us. They encompass our beliefs, attitudes, experiences, and values, shaping how we interpret events and interact with each other.

Imagine standing on a hilltop gazing at a breathtaking landscape. Everyone beside you may see something entirely different, appreciating diverse colors, shapes, and textures. Similarly, our perspectives color our perceptions, guiding our thoughts and influencing our actions.

It's essential to examine the transformative power of perspectives and explore how they can impact your understanding, empathy, and personal growth. By stepping into the shoes of others and embracing different viewpoints, you open doors to new possibilities to enrich your life with compassion and wisdom.

Discover the magic of shifting your perspective and how it empowers you to navigate challenges, celebrate diversity, and cultivate a growth mindset. Through these insights, you will learn to embrace change with an open mind and embrace the ever-evolving beauty of the world through the magical lens of perception.

The Lens of Perception

Our perception is a powerful filter that shapes how we interpret and make sense of the world. It is not merely about seeing with our eyes but involves processing information, drawing conclusions, and attributing meaning to our experiences. Our perception creates a unique and personalized picture of reality, giving sense to the events and interactions in our lives.

Imagine you are meeting someone new for the first time. Your perception of this individual might be influenced by their appearance, body language, and even your mood at the time. If you approach the encounter positively, you may see them as friendly and approachable, opening the door to a potential new friend. However, if you are anxious or have preconceived judgments, your perception might be clouded, and you may miss out on an opportunity to form a meaningful connection.

Now, think about a challenging situation at school. Your perception of the difficulty could impact how you respond to it. If you view the challenge as an opportunity to learn and grow, you might approach it with determination and a growth mindset. This mindset could positively affect your career in the future, as being able to master the problem subject will be a requirement for college later in life.

On the other hand, if you perceive it as impossible, you may feel overwhelmed and discouraged, which could hinder your progress and limit your potential.

The magic of the lens of perception lies in its malleability. With your growth mindset, you can learn to recognize and challenge your ingrained perceptions. By adopting curiosity and open-mindedness, you can expand your perspective, gaining new insights and understanding. As you refine this lens, you can transform your view of the world and your place in it positively.

Embracing the lens of perception empowers you to see beyond the surface, acknowledge different truths, and connect with others at a profound level. It enables you to build bridges of empathy, appreciation, and compassion, transforming your interactions into moments of magic and understanding.

As you embark on this journey of self-awareness and personal growth, open yourself to the wonders of the lens of perception.

> *By cultivating a deeper awareness of how your perception shapes your reality, you can enrich your life with clarity, empathy, and the ability to see the world in all its breathtaking diversity. Through the lens of perception, you unlock the magic of understanding and connect with the deeper layers of life's enchanting tapestry.*

The Power of Positive Thinking

Positive thinking is not merely about wearing rose-colored glasses or denying challenges. It is a mindset that focuses on seeing the good in every situation and believing in the potential for favorable outcomes.

The magic of positive thinking lies in its ability to shape our attitudes and beliefs, influencing our actions and experiences. When we cultivate a positive outlook, we become more resilient in the face of setbacks and challenges. Instead of succumbing to negativity, we rise with determination and hope, embracing the growth journey with an unwavering spirit.

Imagine a situation where you face an important test at school. With a positive thinking mindset, you approach the test as another opportunity to learn and improve. You believe in your abilities and confidently tackle the test, seeking to understand the material rather than fearing failure.

This optimistic perspective not only alleviates stress but also empowers you to perform at your best, unlocking your potential and enabling you to achieve your goals.

The power of positive thinking extends beyond academic activities. It can impact all aspects of your life positively, including relationships, health, and personal well-being. When you adopt positive thinking, you become a beacon of encouragement and support for others, radiating warmth and kindness. Your positive outlook inspires those around you to embrace their strengths and view challenges as stepping stones to growth.

However, positive thinking does not imply avoiding negative emotions or denying hardships. It is about acknowledging the obstacles while maintaining the belief that they can be overcome. You tap into your inner strength by redirecting your focus to solutions and possibilities. Positive thinking enables you to cultivate resilience, creativity, and resourcefulness in the face of adversity.

As you embrace the magic of positive thinking, you awaken your potential and unlock doors to a brighter, more fulfilling future.

Let us journey forward with an optimistic outlook, transforming challenges into stepping stones and weaving a tapestry of positivity in our lives and those around us.

> *Through positive thinking, we harness the power to shape our reality and create a world imbued with hope, resilience, and unwavering determination. With each positive thought and action, we embrace the magic of possibilities and embark on an extraordinary adventure filled with growth, joy, and self-discovery.*

Embracing Change with an Open Mind

Change is a constant and natural part of life, giving us new opportunities and challenges. With an open mind, we welcome change as a gateway to growth, allowing it to shape us into more resilient, adaptable, and empowered individuals.

The magic of embracing change lies in our willingness to explore the unknown and step out of our comfort zones. When we resist change, we may miss out on the wondrous possibilities. However, with an open mind, we can view change as an adventure, each twist and turn leading us to uncharted territories of self-discovery.

Consider a time when you faced a significant change, such as transitioning to a new school or a different city. With an open mind, you approach this change as an opportunity to make new friends, explore new interests, and create new memories. This positive perspective eases the transition and empowers you to embrace the change with excitement and curiosity.

Accepting change with an open mind also allows us to cultivate resilience. Life's journey may present unexpected detours, but an open mind enables us to adapt and bounce back stronger. By letting go of rigid expectations, we can flow with the currents of change, learning valuable life lessons.

While change can be intimidating, it often brings personal growth and transformation. We become more flexible, creative, and resourceful as we embrace change with an open mind. We develop a deeper understanding of ourselves and others, recognizing that change can be an opportunity for collective growth and progress.

When you foster a spirit of openness and curiosity, you unlock the door to a world of endless possibilities, igniting the spark of wonder and discovery in every aspect of your life. With each step, you accept change as a friend and mentor, guiding you toward the bright horizon of your dreams and aspirations. By embracing change with an open mind, you transform challenges into stepping stones and weave a tapestry of resilience and growth that carries you forward on this magical journey of life.

As we finish this chapter about the importance of your perspective, carry the transformative magic of embracing change with an open mind. You have discovered that change is an inevitable companion on your growth journey. With an open mind, you can embark on this life lesson, welcoming change as an opportunity for self-discovery, resilience, and personal transformation.

When you embrace change with an open mind, you have learned to navigate the winds of change with grace and courage. You have accepted change as a gateway to new possibilities, stepping into uncharted territories with excitement and curiosity. By letting go of rigid expectations and fear of the unknown, you have discovered that change can be an adventure filled with wonder and growth.

With each twist and turn, you have found the strength to adapt and bounce back stronger, weaving resilience into the fabric of your being. Embracing change with an open mind has empowered you to embrace life's challenges with optimism and resourcefulness, transforming setbacks into stepping stones on your journey of personal growth.

Always remember that change is not to be feared, for it is through change that you grow, evolve, and become the architect of your destiny. By embracing change with an open mind, you unlock the door to a world of endless possibilities, igniting the spark of wonder and discovery at every step of our magical journey.

> *As you journey forward, carry the magic of change with an open mind into every aspect of your life. Approach each new chapter with an unwavering spirit of openness and curiosity, knowing that change can be a friend and mentor, guiding you toward the bright horizon of your dreams and aspirations.*

As we continue on this adventure of life, let us carry the transformative power of embracing change with an open mind in our hearts. With each change that comes your way, embrace it with optimism and grace, knowing that it is through change that you **discover your most authentic self** and the magic that lies within you.

But what's also so important is how you talk to yourself. It's time to learn all about this in the next chapter, *Positive Self-Talk*.

> "Change the way you look at things,
> and the things you look at change."
> - Wayne Dyer

Chapter 7

Positive Self-Talk

Self-talk is a powerful tool because it shapes our beliefs, emotions, and actions. How we talk to ourselves can significantly influence how we perceive challenges, setbacks, and opportunities. By becoming aware of our self-talk and consciously adopting more positive and empowering language, we can cultivate a growth mindset, boost our self-confidence, and navigate life's challenges with greater resilience and optimism. Practicing positive self-talk can help you develop an attitude of growth, possibility, and self-empowerment, setting the stage for personal growth and success in various areas of life.

What Is Self-Talk?

Self-talk refers to the ongoing internal conversation and thoughts within a person's mind. It is how we talk to ourselves, often happening automatically and unconsciously throughout the day. Self-talk can be positive, negative, or neutral, significantly impacting our emotions, behavior, and overall mindset.

Positive self-talk involves using supportive, encouraging, and optimistic language toward yourself. It can include affirmations, self-encouragement, and reminders of personal strengths and past successes. It helps build self-confidence, resilience, and a growth mindset, as it focuses on possibilities and solutions rather than dwelling on limitations or failures.

Negative self-talk, on the other hand, involves critical, pessimistic, or self-defeating thoughts. This may include self-doubt, self-criticism, and thoughts of inadequacy. This can harm your self-esteem and lead to increased stress, anxiety, and a fixed mindset, where you believe your abilities are limited and unchangeable.

Neutral self-talk is neither positive nor negative and is often based on factual or unbiased observations without judgment. While neutral self-talk doesn't have the same emotional impact as positive or negative self-talk, it can still influence our perceptions and attitudes over time.

The Language of Positivity

As you have already discovered, you have the power within your mind to shape your reality, build confidence, and overcome challenges. Positive self-talk transforms your journey into a tale of courage and triumph. So, in this section, you will learn how positive self-talk will empower you to conquer your doubts and unleash your true potential.

The language of positivity holds the key to unlocking the full potential of your mind. Like a gentle breeze that lifts your spirit, positive words and thoughts can shape your reality and transform your journey into an uplifting tale of courage and resilience.

Harnessing the Power of Positive Words

Like a skilled wordsmith crafting enchanting tales, you can use positive words to inspire and empower yourself. Embrace the uplifting and encouraging language in your thoughts and how you speak to others. Doing so creates a powerful set of beliefs that nurtures your self-esteem and builds a foundation of optimism.

Rewriting Limiting Beliefs

Get into the habit of challenging and rewriting limiting beliefs that might hold you back. Replace thoughts like "I can't" with "I can" and "I don't know" with "I will learn." As you transform your self-talk, you open the door to possibilities and opportunities.

Cultivating a Positive Mindset

A positive mindset is like a radiant sunrise, illuminating your path with hope and possibility. Embrace gratitude and focus on the silver linings, even in challenging situations. By cultivating a positive mindset, you become a master of your thoughts, and your beliefs shape the world you experience.

The Magic of Self-Encouragement

Practice self-encouragement regularly like a kind mentor guiding your way. Celebrate your successes, no matter how small, and offer gentle reassurance during setbacks. By becoming your cheerleader, you cultivate self-compassion and resilience for your journey ahead.

The Power of Kindness in Words

Just as a heartfelt compliment can brighten someone's day, be mindful of the impact your words can have on others. Offer genuine encouragement and support to those around you, as your kindness will ripple throughout your world.

You have discovered that the language of positivity is a spellbinding force that shapes your thoughts and beliefs. Embrace the magic of positive self-talk, and witness how your words and thoughts create a world filled with hope, confidence, and boundless possibilities.

> *As you continue your journey through a growth mindset, let the language of positivity be the guiding star that leads you toward an extraordinary life of courage and triumph.*

Taming the Inner Critic

Every adventurer faces an elusive and formidable foe known as the inner critic. Like a relentless shadow, this internal voice can be harsh and critical, whispering doubts and self-criticism into your mind.

When you listen to this voice, you are holding yourself back from becoming the best version of yourself. Taming the inner critic is the key to unlocking the magic of self-empowerment and building unwavering self-confidence.

Everybody has an inner critic, even your teachers and parents. The good news is that you hold the power over it by deciding how much attention you will give it.

What Is the Inner Critic?

The inner critic is an aspect of your subconscious mind that can manifest as negative thoughts and self-judgment. That nagging voice in your head doubts your abilities, belittles your accomplishments, and emphasizes your mistakes and shortcomings. When faced with challenges or new experiences, the inner critic often emerges, attempting to protect you from potential failures or discomfort.

While the inner critic may have good intentions, it can also hinder your growth and self-confidence. Taming the inner critic involves recognizing its presence, questioning its validity, and replacing negative self-talk with empowering thoughts.

By challenging the inner critic, practicing self-compassion, and embracing imperfections, you reclaim your power and unlock the magic of self-belief and self-empowerment. As you tame the inner critic, you pave the way for growth and self-discovery, where self-compassion and self-confidence become the guiding stars on your journey.

Recognizing the Inner Critic

The first step in taming the inner critic is recognizing its presence. Like a skilled tracker identifying footprints, be aware of the negative self-talk and self-doubt that can cloud your thoughts.

Understand that the inner critic reflects not your true worth but a learned thinking pattern you can unlearn with awareness, focus, and effort. With effort and focus, you can learn new positive thinking patterns.

Challenging Negative Thoughts

As a fearless warrior challenges adversaries, confront your inner critic with courage. When negative thoughts arise, question their validity and challenge them with evidence of your accomplishments and capabilities.

Cultivating Self-Compassion

Treat yourself with kindness and self-compassion. Replace self-criticism with self-understanding and forgiveness. Remember that everyone makes mistakes, and you deserve compassion, just like anyone else.

Embracing Imperfections

In your growth journey, imperfections are not flaws but stepping stones to progress. Like a skillful artist embracing the beauty of imperfections, recognize that you are a work in progress, constantly evolving and learning.

Practicing Positive Affirmations

Affirmations are like empowering spells that counteract the inner critic's negativity. Create positive affirmations that uplift and empower you. Repeat them regularly to weaken the inner critic's grip and replace it with a new sense of self-belief.

Seeking Support from Allies

Seek support from friends, family, or mentors that you trust. Share your struggles with taming the inner critic, and let their encouragement and guidance be a shield against self-doubt.

The Power of Affirmations

The power of affirmations is a mystical force that can transform your thoughts and beliefs. Like ancient incantations manifesting your desires, affirmations are magical spells you craft to ignite self-confidence, positivity, and confidence in your abilities.

Crafting Empowering Affirmations

Like an alchemist concocting the perfect potion, always create affirmations that align with your goals and dreams. Make them personal, positive, and present tense, as if the magic is already unfolding within you. For example, use "I am" followed by a quality you want to see in yourself. For example, "I am brave" or "I am confident."

You will discover more about this in the next chapter, *Affirmations*.

Repetition for Reinforcement

Repetition is the key to reinforcing the magic of affirmations. Like reciting sacred verses, repeat your affirmations regularly, allowing them to seep into your subconscious mind and shape your beliefs.

Visualization and Emotion

Add a touch of enchantment to your affirmations by visualizing your desired outcomes and feeling the emotions that come with achieving them. If you struggle to first see something in your mind, you will probably struggle to achieve it in your life. Let the magic of visualization infuse your affirmations with energy and passion.

Affirmations for Overcoming Challenges

In facing challenges, like a shield of protection, use affirmations to boost your resilience and determination. Affirm your ability to overcome obstacles and grow stronger through adversity. Affirmations can give you the extra boost you need or even calm you when necessary.

Morning and Evening Rituals

Create enchanting rituals by incorporating affirmations into your morning and evening routines. Like sacred chants, let them set the tone for the day ahead and bring peace and gratitude before sleep.

Recording Affirmations

Like preserving ancient wisdom, record your affirmations and listen to them. Hearing your voice reciting positive statements strengthens their impact and makes them an integral part of your magical journey.

Affirmations for Self-Love and Acceptance

As you delve into the wonders of positive self-talk, remember that your mind is a powerful cauldron capable of brewing spells that can change your reality. Embrace the magic of positive thinking, and let it illuminate your path with hope and courage.

> *Embrace the magic of self-love and acceptance by crafting affirmations that honor and celebrate your uniqueness. Affirm your worthiness and embrace yourself as the magical being you are.*

The adventure of a growth mindset continues, and with it, the promise of a journey filled with limitless possibilities.

So, let's now discover more about *Affirmations*.

> *"Positive self-talk can be the spark that ignites the fire of greatness within you."*
> — Anonymous

Chapter 8

Affirmations

"Every day I am becoming the best version of myself."

To start this chapter on Affrmations, I thought it would be a good idea to begin with a simple yet powerful affirmation. Read it out loud and commit it to memory so that you can repeat it every day.

As previously discussed, affirmations are powerful statements that boost your self-confidence, resilience, and optimism. Repeating these statements regularly can shape your beliefs and mindset, creating a more positive and fulfilling life. From building confidence to overcoming challenges, affirmations have the potential to be a valuable tool on your journey of personal growth and self-discovery.

So, let's delve into the realm of affirmations and discover their powerful influence on your thoughts and beliefs.

When to Use Affirmations

You can use affirmations in various situations to help boost your self-confidence, stay motivated, and cultivate a positive mindset. Here are some instances when using affirmations can be beneficial:

Building Confidence

Use affirmations to boost your self-confidence before a challenging task, like taking a test, giving a presentation, or trying something new. Repeating positive statements can help you believe in your abilities and face the situation with courage.

Overcoming Challenges

When faced with obstacles or setbacks, affirmations can help you stay resilient and motivated. You should approach challenges with a positive and determined mindset by reminding yourself of your inner strength and ability to overcome difficulties.

Setting Goals

Affirmations can be powerful tools for setting and achieving goals. By stating your goals in the present tense as if they have already been achieved, you reinforce your belief in your ability to make your dreams a reality.

Promoting Positive Self-Talk

Affirmations help counteract negative self-talk and self-doubt. Replacing self-criticism with self-encouragement can improve self-esteem and develop a positive outlook.

Developing a Growth Mindset

Affirmations can reinforce the belief that people learn and grow through effort and dedication. By adopting a growth mindset, you embrace challenges as opportunities for growth and view failures as stepping stones to success.

Cultivating Self-Love and Acceptance

Affirmations that focus on self-love and acceptance can help you develop a healthier relationship with yourself. They remind you to treat yourself with kindness and compassion, acknowledging your worthiness and uniqueness.

Managing Stress and Anxiety

During stress or anxiety, positive affirmations can help calm your mind and reduce negative thoughts. Repeating calming and reassuring statements can bring a sense of peace and grounding.

Affirmation Examples

Remember that affirmations work best when they are **personal, positive**, and **meaningful** to you. So it's worth putting in a lot of thought about the areas of your life you wish to improve.

They are most effective when used regularly through spoken or written repetition. Affirmations are like magic; they can shape your thoughts and beliefs, empowering you to create a more positive and fulfilling life.

Below are some simple affirmations that you can use to get started:

Building Confidence

1. I am confident and capable of handling any challenge that comes my way.

2. I believe in myself and my abilities to succeed.

3. I am well-prepared, and I trust in my preparation.

4. I dare to face anything with a positive attitude.

5. I am strong, and I can handle anything that comes my way.

Overcoming Challenges

1. I embrace any challenges as opportunities for growth and learning.

2. I am resilient, and I bounce back from setbacks with determination.

3. Every challenge I encounter makes me stronger and wiser.

4. I am capable of finding creative and workable solutions to any obstacle.

5. I face challenges with confidence and a positive mindset.

Setting Goals

1. I am focused and am determined to achieve my goals.

2. I am deserving of success, and I am attracting positive outcomes.

3. I am making steady progress toward my dreams.

4. I achieve my goals with ease and joy.

5. I believe in myself and my ability to reach my goals.

Promoting Positive Self-Talk

1. I am worthy of love and acceptance just as I am.
2. I am kind to myself and treat myself with compassion.
3. My mistakes do not define me; I learn and grow from them.
4. I have the power to choose positive thoughts and beliefs.
5. I am confident in my abilities and trust in my judgment.

Developing a Growth Mindset

1. I can learn and improve through practice and effort.
2. Challenges help me grow and become a better version of myself.
3. I am not afraid of making mistakes as they are part of learning.
4. I embrace new opportunities and challenges with excitement.
5. I believe in my potential to achieve anything I set my mind to.

Cultivating Self-Love and Acceptance

1. I love and accept myself unconditionally.
2. I am worthy of love, acceptance, and respect from myself and others.
3. I am unique, and I celebrate my individuality.
4. I am deserving of happiness and kindness.
5. I treat myself with love and care, just like a dear friend.

Managing Stress and Anxiety

1. I am calm and easily handle stress.

2. I release tension and stress from my body and mind.

3. I am in control of my thoughts and emotions.

4. I breathe deeply and stay centered during challenging moments.

5. I trust in my ability to handle stressful situations with grace and composure.

Affirmations are personal and should resonate with you. Feel free to modify or create your own affirmations that align with your unique goals and aspirations. Repeating these affirmations regularly infuses your mind with positive beliefs that will transform your reality and empower you on your magical journey of growth and self-discovery.

Situational Affirmations

Situation: Failing a Test
I am capable of learning and improving. One test does not define my intelligence or worth. I will study harder and improve next time.

Situation: Facing Bullying or Teasing
I am strong and resilient. I deserve to be treated with kindness, care and respect. I will stand up for myself and speak up if someone is unkind to me.

Situation: Not Getting Picked for a Team
I am unique and valuable, no matter the team or activity I'm part of. I will keep trying to find a way to bring out my best.

Situation: Feeling Overwhelmed with Schoolwork
I am capable of managing my time and tasks. I will take one step at a time and ask for help if needed. With effort and focus, I can accomplish my goals.

Situation: Making a Mistake in Front of Classmates
Mistakes are a natural part of learning and growing. I am brave, and I learn from my mistakes. I won't let fear hold me back from trying again.

Situation: Feeling Left Out in a New School
I am a unique and valuable individual. Making new friends takes time, and I am confident that I will find true friends who appreciate me for who I am. I will be kind and open to others, knowing that meaningful friendships will come my way.

Remember, affirmations are powerful tools that shift your negative to a positive mindset. Repeat these affirmations regularly, write them down, and create a positive affirmation poster to hang in your room. With the magic of affirmations, you can build confidence, resilience, and a growth mindset that will guide you through any challenge you may face.

Below are two longer affirmations, one for the morning and one for nighttime. Feel free to change them and create your own.

Lifelong Morning Affirmation

This affirmation is a powerful reminder for every morning, setting the tone for the day ahead. By repeating this positive statement, you reinforce the belief in your potential and ability to improve continuously. It encourages you to approach each day with an open mind, embracing challenges as opportunities for growth.

As you start your day with this affirmation, you remind yourself that no matter the circumstances, you can learn, adapt, and overcome any challenges that come your way. Your past or current abilities do not limit you; you are empowered to develop new skills, gain knowledge, and become a better version of yourself.

> *I am capable, worthy, and full of potential. Today, I embrace challenges as opportunities to learn and grow. I will face the day with courage, kindness, and determination. I am the master of my mindset and choose to create a positive, successful, and fulfilling today.*

By instilling this lifelong affirmation into your morning routine, you cultivate a growth mindset that will guide you throughout your life's journey. Repeating this each morning, you will start your day with a renewed sense of purpose and determination to embrace the magic of growth and self-discovery.

Keep this affirmation close to your heart, and watch as it empowers you to create a life filled with endless possibilities and achievements.

Lifelong Nighttime Affirmation

Nighttime affirmations offer the benefits of promoting relaxation, fostering a positive mindset, and reinforcing empowering beliefs in the subconscious mind, ultimately leading to improved sleep quality, reduced stress, and a more optimistic outlook that extends into the following day.

> *I am proud of the efforts I made and the lessons I learned today. Tomorrow is a new opportunity, and I look forward to embracing it with curiosity and an open heart. I am resilient and capable of facing any challenges that come my way. As I rest, I know I am a unique and amazing individual, ready to dream big and make tomorrow even better.*

Remember, the effectiveness of affirmations may vary from person to person. Choosing affirmations that resonate with you and align with your goals and aspirations is important. Over time, consistent practice can help you create a more positive and empowered mindset, contributing to a fulfilling and joyful life.

Now that you understand affirmations, let's move on to *The Power of YET*.

> *"Challenges are what make life interesting and overcoming them is what makes life meaningful."*
> *- Joshua J. Marine*

Chapter 9

The Power of YET

YET holds the key to unlocking your true potential, reminding you that every skill and achievement takes time and effort to master. You will discover that growth and learning are continuous, like a blossoming flower. With determination and a positive attitude, it is possible to turn "I can't" into "I can!" In this chapter, we will explore the captivating world of YET, where every step forward becomes a testament to your magical growth.

I Can't Do It YET

Once upon a time, a young fairy named Julia lived in an enchanted land far away. Julia loved to explore the magical forest and dreamt of becoming the best flyer in the fairy kingdom. However, she often felt discouraged, for her wings were not as strong as those of her fairy friends.

One day, while watching her friends soar gracefully through the sky, Julia sighed and said, "I can't fly as high as they do." But then, a wise elder fairy named Catherine overheard her and gently said, "Ah, my dear Julia, you can't fly as high YET, but with practice and determination, you will."

Catherine told Julia about the power of "I can't do it YET" and how it was a magical phrase that held the promise of growth and learning. "Every fairy starts by flapping their wings just like you, but with time and effort, they become stronger fliers," said Catherine. "You, too, have the magic within you to become a great flyer!"

Encouraged by Catherine's wisdom, Julia began her journey of growth. She practiced flying every day, flapping her wings with determination. Sometimes, she stumbled, and other times, she felt tired, but she never gave up. Whenever she felt discouraged, she reminded herself, "I can't fly as high YET, but I will get there with practice."

Julia's wings strengthened as the days turned into weeks, and as her confidence soared, so did her ability to fly. She began to fly higher and faster than ever before. The other fairies cheered her progress and praised her perseverance.

One sunny morning, when the fairy kingdom was celebrating a special event, Julia decided to show her newfound flying skills. With a determined sparkle in her eyes, she flapped her wings and soared gracefully through the sky, performing daring loops and twists.

The fairies below gasped in awe at Julia's breathtaking display. Julia beamed joyfully, knowing she had turned "**I can't do it YET**" into "**I can do it NOW!**"

From that day on, Julia continued to grow and learn, knowing there was no limit to what she could achieve with a growth mindset. Every challenge became an opportunity to improve, and she moved closer to achieving her dreams through every setback.

Always remember the tale of Julia, the fairy who learned the magic of "I can't do it YET."

> *Embrace challenges with a positive mindset, for every "I can't" holds the promise of growth and potential. With perseverance and belief in yourself, you can turn "I can't" into "I can!"*

Your growth journey awaits you, and the magic of "I can't do it YET" will guide you toward wondrous possibilities and extraordinary achievements.

The Transformative Effect of Yet

Like a magical key that unlocks hidden potential, the tiny word YET, with its transformative power to turn "I can't" into "I can," introduces a world of possibilities and learning opportunities.

Embracing the Journey of Growth

When we say, "I can't do it," it closes the door to progress. We are telling ourselves that it is pointless even to try.

We have given up.

However, by adding the little word YET to the end of our statement, we open ourselves up to a journey of growth and improvement. "I can't do it YET" becomes a promise that with dedication and effort, we can overcome any challenge.

Cultivating Resilience and Perseverance

The magic of YET teaches us that setbacks are not permanent. Instead of feeling defeated, we must embrace resilience and perseverance, knowing our limitations are only temporary. With a growth mindset, we view failures as opportunities to learn and grow stronger.

Turning Obstacles into Stepping Stones

"I can't do it YET" empowers us to see obstacles as stepping stones to success. Each challenge becomes a chance to develop new skills and gain valuable experiences. As we navigate through difficulties with a positive outlook, we build confidence in our ability to overcome future obstacles.

Fostering a Positive Attitude

The power of YET nurtures a positive attitude towards learning and improvement. Instead of feeling discouraged by initial difficulties, we embrace a sense of possibility and curiosity. With an optimistic mindset, we enthusiastically approach new tasks and are eager to explore.

Embracing a Growth Mindset

Including YET transforms our mindset from fixed to growth-oriented. Our abilities can be developed through dedication and practice. This growth mindset encourages us to take on challenges, seek feedback, and continuously strive for improvement.

Celebrating Progress and Effort

With the magic of YET, you can acknowledge your progress and effort rather than focusing only on the result. This also helps you focus on the journey, allowing you to enjoy it instead of just focusing on the end result. Each step forward, no matter how small, becomes a cause for celebration.

Unlocking Hidden Potential

"I can't do it YET" reveals your untapped potential and reminds you that growth has no limits. The word YET ignites the spark of belief in your ability to achieve greatness, and you realize that you can shape your reality and accomplish extraordinary feats.

> *When you say YET, every challenge becomes an opportunity, every setback a chance to grow, and every effort a step toward mastery. With this transformative word, your journey of self-discovery and magical growth turns "I can't" into an empowering "I can!"*

Start using the magic of YET today, and witness the incredible transformation when you believe in your limitless potential.

Embracing the Journey of Learning

Your learning journey is a magical adventure with wondrous discoveries and exciting possibilities. Embracing this journey means embracing the art of continuous growth and improvement, where every step becomes a testament to your curiosity and dedication.

Curiosity Unleashed

With a growth mindset, curiosity becomes your guiding compass. You embark on a quest to explore and learn about the world around you. Like a dedicated explorer, you ask questions, seek answers, and dive fearlessly into obtaining new knowledge.

Embracing Challenges

Challenges become invitations rather than roadblocks on this journey. Instead of shying away from difficulties, you embrace them enthusiastically, knowing they are only stepping stones to learning and growth, and with each stone you step over, you will be one step closer to success.

Celebrating Progress

Each milestone, no matter how small, is a cause for celebration. As you learn and progress, acknowledge your efforts and see mistakes as valuable lessons that pave the way for your improvement.

Effort Is the Magic Ingredient

On this journey, effort becomes the magical ingredient that turns potential into reality. You understand that dedication and hard work are the keys to unlocking your potential to achieve greatness.

Embracing the Unknown

With a growth mindset, you step boldly into the unknown, knowing that every new experience brings opportunities to learn and expand your horizons. You are not afraid to take risks and try new things.

Transforming Failure into Wisdom

On your learning journey, failure is not a dead end but a detour that leads to wisdom. Each setback becomes a valuable lesson that guides you toward success.

Learning as a Lifelong Adventure

With a growth mindset, learning becomes a lifelong adventure. You realize there is always more to discover, and the quest for knowledge never ends. Every day presents new opportunities to learn and grow.

The power of YET lies in the capability to change your mindset from being fixed into a growth mindset, unleashing the magic of possibility and potential. Adding YET to the end of a statement like "I can't do it" changes the meaning from limitation to growth and progress.

In a fixed mindset, people believe their abilities are fixed traits that cannot be changed. When faced with challenges or setbacks, they may easily give up, feeling defeated and thinking, "I can't do it." This fixed mindset can hinder personal growth and limit opportunities for learning and development.

However, YET introduces a growth mindset based on the belief that abilities can be developed through effort, dedication, and learning. Instead of viewing challenges as roadblocks, individuals with a growth mindset see them as stepping stones toward improvement.

When they encounter obstacles and say, "I can't do it yet," they acknowledge that they haven't mastered the skill or task YET, but they have the potential to do so in the future.

The word YET is a magical reminder that progress and success are not instant but take time and effort. It instills hope and a sense of possibility, encouraging individuals to persevere and keep trying.

With a growth mindset, individuals are more likely to embrace challenges, learn from mistakes, and view effort as a necessary part of the learning process.

Incorporating YET into your vocabulary opens you up to growth and transformation. It empowers you to approach challenges with optimism and resilience, knowing you continuously improve.

> *Embracing the power of YET allows you to see yourself not as a fixed being with limitations but as an ever-evolving being with limitless potential.*

As you embrace the learning journey with a growth mindset, you become a magical seeker of knowledge, constantly evolving and expanding your understanding of the world.

Every experience becomes a stepping stone on this wondrous path, and every moment is a chance to unlock your true potential. With curiosity as your wand and dedication as your spell, you embark on a journey where **learning becomes a source of joy** and empowerment.

As with any magic potion, there's usually a secret ingredient, and developing a growth mindset is no different.

But what is the secret ingredient?

> *"I can't change the direction of the wind,
> but I can adjust my sails to always reach my destination."*
> *- Jimmy Dean*

Chapter 10

The Secret Ingredient

When you look at the picture above, can you sense the effort it takes to push that ball up the hill? Would you make that effort if it was important to get the ball to the top?

You've guessed it – the secret ingredient is **effort**!

In this chapter, you will uncover the powerful role of effort in achieving success and making magic happen in your life.

An effort is the dedicated energy we invest in pursuing our goals and dreams. It is the driving force behind progress and growth, which empowers us to overcome challenges and obstacles. The effort is not about relying solely on talents or abilities but the willingness to try, learn, and persevere even when faced with difficulties.

Making an effort can be challenging at times. We may encounter setbacks, doubts, and moments of exhaustion where we must step out of our comfort zones, face our fears, and put in the time and hard work. However, in these moments of struggle, we often discover our true potential and the depth of our determination.

Despite the challenges, the rewards of making an effort are immeasurable. The effort allows us to improve, learn new skills, and reach heights we once thought impossible. It instills in us a sense of pride and accomplishment, knowing that we have given our best to achieve our goals. Effort also strengthens our character, fostering resilience and a growth mindset that can serve us throughout life.

Throughout this chapter, you will learn that success is not just about natural talents but the effort we invest in honing our skills and pushing ourselves beyond our limits. Whether learning a new spell, mastering a craft, or pursuing a dream, effort is the secret ingredient that can turn ordinary actions into extraordinary achievements.

So, let's delve into the world of effort and discover how it can unlock the door to accomplishment and make our magical journey even more rewarding. Get ready to embrace the power of inspired action and witness its transformative impact on your life.

An Extraordinary Story

A young boy named Thomas lived in a bustling town set between rolling hills. Thomas was no ordinary child. His insatiable curiosity led him on adventures beyond the familiar paths. One morning, as he explored the woods near his home, he stumbled upon an old oak tree with branches that reached for the sky like outstretched arms. He had never seen this unique tree before.

Intrigued, Thomas decided to climb the tree. At first, his progress was slow and cautious, like any ordinary child. But as he climbed higher, something extraordinary happened. Thomas began to notice the delicate dance of leaves in the breeze, the soft rustle of squirrels scurrying about, and how the world below seemed to shrink as he got higher.

Thomas reached a sturdy branch and settled himself among the leaves. From this new vantage point, the town looked like a miniature village, and the hills stretched like an endless painting. As he gazed at the world, Thomas realized that being extraordinary required more than just being ordinary – it demanded an extra effort, a willingness to go beyond what most would do.

With this newfound insight, Thomas didn't stop at the branch where he rested. He continued to climb, pushing his limits and testing his boundaries. He scrambled up high, navigating the rough bark with determination. With each step, he marveled at the extraordinary view unfolding before him.

As the sun climbed higher in the sky, so did Thomas until he reached the very top of the tree. His heart swelled with a sense of accomplishment and wonder. He had ventured beyond the ordinary, making the extra effort to reach this extraordinary height even though he had felt tired. From his lofty perch, Thomas understood that the world held endless opportunities for those who dared to do more, to strive for the extraordinary.

With a contented smile, Thomas began to climb down, knowing that his climb had not only taken him to new heights but had also taught him a valuable lesson. To be extraordinary meant embracing the challenge of going beyond what seemed possible, putting in the extra effort many other kids might shy away from. As he returned to the ground, Thomas learned that being extraordinary was a choice to stretch, grow, and reach for the extraordinary in every corner of his life.

To be extraordinary, he would have to make the effort to go beyond the ordinary!

Please note I am not suggesting you go out and climb the highest tree you can find. The story above is just a story to highlight the differences between making the extra effort and not making an effort at all.

Making Practice Fun and Effective

Practice is the key that unlocks our hidden potential and allows us to reach new heights of skill and ability. This enables you to refine your skills to excel in your chosen pursuits through dedicated effort and repetition.

While practice may sometimes seem repetitive or monotonous, it doesn't have to be that way. Practice can be an exciting journey of discovery and growth, filled with moments of joy and satisfaction.

Imagine yourself perfecting a new skill and confidently navigating challenges with ease. Picture yourself honing your abilities and reaching new proficiency levels with each session.

These moments of progress and improvement are not solely the result of talent but are achieved through purposeful and enjoyable practice.

Each practice session will take you one step closer to achieving your full potential and success in your chosen pursuits. To make practice enjoyable and purposeful, follow the tips below.

And remember, practice takes effort. This includes the actual practice session as well as your attitude towards it.

Set Exciting Goals

Set specific and exciting goals for your practice sessions. Whether perfecting a spell or improving your wand techniques, having clear objectives will keep you focused and motivated.

Break It Down

Divide your practice into smaller, manageable chunks. This way, you can concentrate on mastering one aspect at a time, making progress more achievable and satisfying. It's easier to accomplish a small task than a big one.

.Use Creative Techniques

Spice up your practice routine with creative techniques. Try role-playing or imagining challenging scenarios to make your training more engaging and immersive.

Gamify Your Practice

Turn practice into a game by setting challenges and rewarding yourself for meeting them. When you have fun and enjoy yourself, you are more likely to make progress. Consider keeping a magical journal to track your progress and celebrate each milestone.

Embrace the Power of Music

Incorporate magical melodies into your practice sessions. Music can enhance concentration and create an uplifting atmosphere, making your practice feel like a captivating adventure.

Collaborate and Learn

Practice with friends to exchange knowledge and learn from one another. Sharing insights and supporting each other can add a social and enjoyable element to your training.

Keep It Fresh

Vary your practice routine to avoid monotony. Get creative and explore new things, techniques, or exercises regularly, and your journey to mastery will be filled with excitement and curiosity. This way, your practice sessions will be something you look forward to instead of a chore to be completed.

Celebrate Your Efforts

Acknowledge your hard work and effort during practice. Treat yourself to small rewards or moments of relaxation as you progress on your magical journey.

> *By infusing fun and creativity into your practice, you'll progress faster and cultivate a passion for learning. Remember, it's not just about the end result; it's about the joy of the journey and the dedication to honing your skills.*

Embracing Challenges as Exciting Adventures

Imagine you are a daring explorer on a thrilling quest to uncover hidden mysteries and conquer uncharted territories. Each challenge you encounter becomes an exciting adventure, offering opportunities for growth, learning, and triumph. Embracing challenges as exciting adventures means seeing obstacles not as roadblocks but as stepping stones that lead you to extraordinary achievements.

We will delve into the mindset of adventurers who thrive in the face of challenges. They demonstrate resilience, adaptability, and an unwavering belief in their abilities. By adopting these qualities, you will embark on your quests with newfound courage and a willingness to embrace the unknown.

So, put on your explorer's hat, grab your trusty map, and prepare to see challenges in a new light. Exciting adventures await you, where every difficulty becomes an opportunity for exploration and growth. Let's journey together and discover the magic within the challenges we encounter!

Below are some examples of embracing challenges:

Conquering Uncharted Lands

Imagine you are an intrepid explorer setting sail on a daring voyage to uncharted lands. Instead of fearing the vast ocean and unknown territories, you enthusiastically embrace the adventure. Each hurdle you face, be it rough waves or unfamiliar landscapes, becomes a thrilling opportunity to discover new cultures, wildlife, and breathtaking vistas.

Scaling Towering Peaks

Picture yourself as a brave mountaineer ascending a towering peak. Instead of dreading the steep slopes and icy winds, you view the challenge as an exhilarating expedition.

Every step you take toward the summit is a testament to your resilience and determination, rewarding you with panoramic views and a sense of accomplishment.

Unraveling Ancient Riddles

Envision yourself as a keen-eyed archaeologist delving into ancient ruins. Rather than feeling overwhelmed by the ancient hieroglyphics and hidden chambers, you embrace the puzzle-solving challenge with curiosity. Each deciphered riddle and uncovered artifact brings you closer to unlocking the secrets of an ancient civilization.

Charting a New Course

Imagine you are a fearless navigator leading your crew on an expedition to discover unexplored islands. Instead of fearing the unknown waters and uncharted maps, you approach the journey as a thrilling opportunity for discovery.

Each decision you make, and obstacle you navigate becomes a step toward mapping new territories and leaving a legacy of exploration.

Escaping a Hidden Temple

Picture yourself as a daring adventurer venturing into a mysterious temple filled with puzzles and traps. Rather than fearing the dangers, you embrace the challenge with a sense of adventure. Each puzzle you solve and trap you evade becomes a triumph, leading you closer to the temple's ancient treasures.

Like explorers, you can approach challenges with the same spirit of adventure and curiosity. Whether facing academic tests, learning new skills, or overcoming personal obstacles, embracing challenges allows you to grow, learn, and explore the uncharted territories of your abilities.

> *So, always keep in mind that putting in effort is a bit like deciding to put extra toppings on your ice cream cone. It might demand a little more time and work, yet the end result becomes incredibly fulfilling and rewarding.*

Just as a skilled wizard hones their spellcraft or a superhero dedicates time to training for their heroic feats, your continuous efforts contribute to your growth, both in strength and intelligence. Keep embracing challenges with determination.

Sooner than you think, you'll become an expert at exerting effort, transforming obstacles into personal triumphs, and forging your path to success!

Now that you understand the significance of effort, let's put that effort into *Creating a Growth Mindset Environment*!

> *"Your beliefs become your thoughts,*
> *your thoughts become your words, your words become your actions,*
> *your actions become your habits, your habits become your values,*
> *and your values become your destiny."*
> \- Mahatma Gandhi

Chapter 11

Creating a Growth Mindset Environment

An environment that encourages positivity and learning to embrace challenges is crucial for a growth mindset to thrive. Let's now explore the powerful impact of our surroundings on nurturing a growth mindset by delving into the practical aspects of shaping such an environment at home and in other settings like schools and communities.

Imagine a place where everyone believes in the potential for growth and improvement. It is a space where effort is valued, mistakes are stepping stones to success, and each person's unique abilities are celebrated.

You will uncover the essential ingredients to cultivate a growth mindset environment. From the power of encouragement and constructive feedback to the importance of inspiring role models, you will discover how each element contributes to nurturing a growth-oriented culture.

In addition, we will discover the role of language and the stories we tell each other in shaping our mindsets. By cultivating positive self-talk and encouraging resilience, we create an environment where growth and progress become the norm.

By the end of this chapter, you will have the tools to transform your surroundings into a growth mindset haven, inspiring yourself and those around you.

So, together, let's embark on this enlightening journey of creating a growth mindset environment where the seeds of potential are nurtured and bloom into extraordinary achievements.

Encouraging Supportive Friendships

The significance of supporting our friends and its profound impact on fostering a growth mindset cannot be underestimated. Just as we thrive in an atmosphere of encouragement and positivity, our friends also draw strength and inspiration from our support.

By uplifting and celebrating their efforts, we create a ripple effect of motivation and belief in their abilities.

When we cultivate a culture of support and encouragement among friends, it paves the way for reciprocity, where they, in turn, offer us the same level of encouragement and belief in our potential.

This cycle of support becomes the very cornerstone of a growth mindset environment, where everyone flourishes and accomplishes their goals with the unwavering support of their friends.

As we explore the practical ways to encourage supportive friendships, we unlock the key to empowering each other's growth and creating a nurturing community of achievement and self-belief.

Supportive friendships are essential in our journey of personal growth and development. When friends believe in and encourage us, we feel more motivated to take on challenges and strive for improvement.

Here are some practical ways to encourage supportive friendships:

Celebrate Efforts

Acknowledge and celebrate each other's efforts, whether trying out a new skill, studying for an upcoming test, or working on a project. Recognizing the hard work and dedication to pursuing goals fosters a growth-oriented mindset.

Provide Constructive Feedback

Offer constructive feedback in a kind and supportive manner. Focus on areas of improvement while highlighting strengths and progress made. Constructive feedback helps friends learn from mistakes and grow.

Share Inspirations

Share stories of growth and success to inspire and motivate each other. Discussing the journeys of others who have overcome challenges can ignite a belief in the possibility of personal growth.

Be Empathetic

Show empathy and understanding when friends face setbacks or difficulties. Remind them that setbacks are part of the learning process and offer encouragement to keep going. Put yourself in their shoes and always treat others how you would like to be treated.

Set Shared Goals

Set shared goals with friends and work together to achieve them. Having common objectives creates a sense of camaraderie and accountability to stay committed to growth.

Provide Encouragement

Offer encouragement and support when facing challenges or stepping out of your comfort zone. A simple "You've got this!" can boost confidence and motivation.

Create a Safe Space

Foster an open, non-judgmental environment where friends feel comfortable sharing their dreams, fears, and aspirations. When you are vulnerable with each other, this allows for deeper connections and growth.

Offer Resources and Help

Share resources, tips, or knowledge to aid each other's growth journey. Helping friends access valuable tools and information can accelerate progress.

These practical steps strengthen our connections with friends and cultivate a growth mindset that thrives in a community of encouragement and support.

> *Encouraging supportive friendships creates a positive and empowering environment where personal growth is embraced and celebrated.*

Nurturing a Growth Mindset at Home

Nurturing a growth mindset within the familiar walls of our homes is significant. Our home environment is central in shaping our beliefs and attitudes, making it a powerful space to foster a growth-oriented mindset.

At home, we find the foundation for our journey of growth and self-discovery. When parents, siblings, and caregivers demonstrate a growth mindset, it sets a powerful example for us to follow. Our home becomes a haven of encouragement and positivity by celebrating effort, valuing resilience, and embracing challenges.

Nurturing a growth mindset at home is essential not only for individual growth but also for the collective well-being of the family. As family members support and inspire each other's aspirations, they form a strong support network that propels everyone toward success.

The role of parents and caregivers in encouraging a growth mindset in their children is vital. By providing constructive feedback, offering praise for effort, and encouraging a love of learning, parents create an environment where children feel empowered to take on challenges and explore their potential.

In addition, family discussions and shared experiences become opportunities for learning and growth. Family members cultivate resilience by openly discussing setbacks and failures as part of the learning journey and embracing the idea that development requires continuous effort.

In this section, you will uncover practical ways to nurture a growth mindset at home. From fostering a positive and encouraging atmosphere to instilling a love for learning and curiosity, we will explore how the warmth and support of home can be harnessed to create a growth-oriented environment.

By nurturing a growth mindset at home, we plant the seeds of self-belief and determination, empowering each family member to flourish and achieve their dreams. Our home environment shapes our beliefs and attitudes, making it a powerful space to foster a growth-oriented mindset.

Below are some practical ways to nurture a growth mindset at home:

Encourage Effort and Progress

Celebrate the effort made by family members, whether a school project, a hobby, or trying something new. Focus on the progress made rather than solely on the result. Acknowledging and praising effort cultivates a belief that improvement is attainable through effort and dedication.

Embrace Challenges Together

Encourage family members to take on challenges and view them as opportunities for growth. Share stories of personal challenges and how they were overcome, emphasizing that mistakes are part of the learning process. Create an environment where taking risks is valued and celebrated.

Model a Growth Mindset

Encourage your family members at home by showing how you keep a growth mindset in your own life. Tell them how you've learned to handle stuff that gets in your way. We want them to see that it's okay to have hiccups sometimes and that not giving up is super important when trying to reach your goals.

Your parents or caregivers will be happy to see you demonstrating a growth mindset in your pursuits, and this will help ensure you continue to have a growth mindset at home and give them confidence in your maturity.

Foster a Love for Learning

Create a culture of curiosity and learning at home. Talk about books, educational resources, and activities that spark interest. Engage in discussions about various topics and encourage questioning and exploration. Watch documentaries on interesting subjects together and discuss your thoughts about what you learned.

Offer Constructive Feedback

When providing feedback to family members, focus on specific areas for improvement rather than criticism. You may have siblings that look to you for guidance. Offer suggestions for overcoming challenges and growing to create an environment where feedback is viewed as an opportunity for learning and development.

Encourage Goal Setting

Help family members set achievable and meaningful goals by learning how to break down larger goals into smaller steps that are simpler to manage and celebrating each milestone reached. Goal setting instills a sense of purpose and direction in pursuing growth.

Cultivate a Positive Atmosphere

Foster a positive and encouraging atmosphere at home. Encourage family members to support and uplift each other's endeavors. Practice gratitude and recognize each other's strengths and achievements.

Emphasize the Learning Process

Remind family members that learning is a continuous journey, and mastery takes time. Encourage a growth mindset by praising perseverance and resilience in facing challenges.

By implementing these practical ways to nurture a growth mindset at home, a supportive and empowering environment is created where family members feel inspired to embrace challenges and strive for continuous improvement. The home becomes a place where the magic of growth and self-belief thrives, empowering each family member to flourish and achieve their dreams.

Building a Growth Mindset Classroom

Your classroom can be a special place where you can believe in yourself and grow more competent daily!

Imagine a classroom focused on a growth mindset.

In this classroom, mistakes are not viewed as failures but rather as learning opportunities to improve. Here, you will learn to embrace challenges and see them as exciting adventures that help you become a stronger learner.

With a growth mindset, you can confidently ask questions or share your ideas. You know that learning is a journey, and it's okay to take your time and keep improving.

Your teacher will be your biggest cheerleader, encouraging you to believe in yourself and celebrate your progress. You'll also be surrounded by supportive friends who lift and inspire you to keep going.

Together, you'll create a positive and inclusive classroom where everyone's unique strengths are valued and where you learn from each other's experiences.

So prepare for an amazing journey of building a growth mindset classroom. Grow and learn together and become the confident and capable learners you were born to be!

A growth mindset classroom is super important because it helps you become confident and resilient learners. Here are some practical steps and examples of how you can create this magical space together:

Talk to Your Teacher

You can start by discussing creating a growth mindset classroom with your teacher. You can share how learning about a growth mindset makes you feel excited and motivated to learn. Your teacher might be thrilled to have the class join you on this journey!

Embrace Challenges

Instead of feeling scared of challenges, you'll see them as exciting opportunities to learn and improve. For example, when you face a tricky math problem, you'll say, "I'll give it my best shot, and even if I don't get it right now, I'll learn from my mistakes and try again." Encourage your classmates to do the same.

Celebrate Effort

Your teacher will understand the importance of praising effort. For example, when you work on a science project, your teacher might say, "I'm proud of how you researched and tried different experiments. Your effort really shows!"

Use Positive Language

Instead of saying, "I can't do it," you'll say, "I can't do it YET." Explain the significance of the little word "yet" to your classmates so they, too, can understand that it can improve with practice. For example, if they struggle with spelling, they'll say, "I can't spell that word yet, but I'll practice and get better."

Learn from Mistakes

Mistakes are part of learning, and show your classmates how to embrace them as valuable lessons. When they make a mistake, they'll learn to say, "Oops, I made a mistake, but that's okay. I'll figure out what went wrong and do better next time."

Support Each Other

Supporting friends, cheering each other on, and helping each other when things get tough. For example, if a friend feels discouraged about a challenging assignment, say, "You've got this! I believe in you, and I'm here to help if you need it." You will get the same support from your friends when you do this.

Set Goals and Track Progress

Discuss setting goals for yourselves and breaking them down into smaller steps. Keep track of progress and celebrate each milestone achieved. For example, if you want to read more books, you'll aim to read one book each week and mark your progress on a chart.

Learn from Role Models

Learn from inspiring people who have faced challenges and never gave up. Read stories of famous scientists, artists, writers, and athletes who worked hard to achieve their dreams.

> *By following these practical steps and talking to your teacher about creating a growth mindset classroom, you'll create a space where you all believe in yourselves, embrace challenges, and know that you can achieve anything with effort and determination.*

So, as we wrap up this chapter on creating a growth mindset environment, remember that you have the incredible power to **shape your own way of thinking**. Embracing challenges, learning from mistakes, and believing in your own potential are like keys to unlocking a treasure trove of possibilities.

With your determination and the support of those around you, you're building a foundation for a mindset that will help you conquer new horizons. Keep nurturing your growth mindset, and prepare for a continuous learning journey and endless growth!

Now, it's time to take a closer look at *The Magic of Failure and Feedback*.

> *"The greatest discovery of all time is that a person can change their future by merely changing their attitude."*
> - Oprah Winfrey

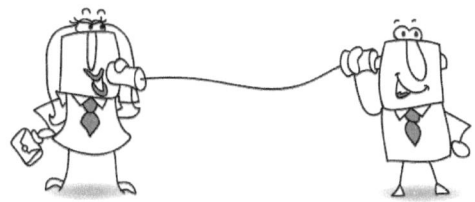

Chapter 12

The Magic of Failure and Feedback

In this chapter, we'll look more deeply into how failure and feedback are not to be feared but embraced as powerful tools for growth and learning.

Sometimes, we feel disappointed or discouraged when things don't go as planned. But don't worry because, as previously mentioned, failure is not the end of the road! Instead, it's an opportunity to learn, adapt, and discover our hidden strengths.

If you've ever felt disheartened when you've failed at something or been upset when others have pointed out what you could have done differently, then this chapter is for you.

I remember once giving constructive feedback to a friend who promptly burst into tears when she heard what I had to say. Of course, it had never been my intention to upset her, but only to help her. Unfortunately, she did not understand the importance of feedback and how it should be received.

We often hear that failure is a bad thing to avoid at all costs. But as you now know, failure is a stepping stone to success., and it should be seen as an opportunity to learn and improve.

This is only possible when you see it with a growth mindset. Failure becomes a magical teacher, guiding us toward our goals with valuable lessons and insights.

Feedback is like a secret map, showing you how to become a better learner and individual.

Feedback is not about criticism but helpful advice and support to help us grow. With feedback, we can fine-tune our skills, refine our understanding, and soar to new heights of achievement.

Together, we'll uncover the magic of viewing failure and feedback as stepping stones to success. You'll learn how to bounce back, use feedback to your advantage, and celebrate the growth from embracing these magical experiences.

The Truth about Failure

This section will uncover the truth about failure and dispel any misconceptions. Failure is an inevitable part of life, and it happens to everyone, including the most successful people in the world. Successful people did not give up when they failed but instead used the knowledge they learned to succeed.

Here are some essential facts about failure:

Failure Is a Natural Process

Failure is a natural part of the learning and growing process. When we try new things and take on challenges, we might only sometimes succeed on the first try. It's essential to recognize that failure is a normal and expected part of any journey toward success. It's certainly better to try and fail than not try at all.

Failure Is a Learning Opportunity

Instead of seeing failure as a dead end, we can view it as an opportunity to learn and improve. Each failure provides valuable insights and teaches us what doesn't work, guiding us toward better approaches and solutions.

Failure Helps Us Build Resilience

When we encounter failure, we can tap into resilience, which is our ability to bounce back from any setbacks. Embracing failure and persevering through challenges make us stronger and better equipped to handle future difficulties.

Failure Is Not a Reflection of Our Worth

Failing at something doesn't make us less capable or valuable as individuals. It's essential to separate our self-worth from our failures and recognize that everyone makes mistakes or faces setbacks from time to time.

It only means that we have not yet learned to master that particular skill or ability, YET!

Successful People Embrace Failure

Many successful individuals achieve greatness by learning from their failures. They view failure as part of the journey to success and use it as a tool for growth and improvement.

Failure Leads to Innovation

Some of the most groundbreaking inventions and discoveries resulted from initial failures. Embracing failure fosters creativity and encourages us to think outside the box to find innovative solutions.

Fear of Failure Holds Us Back

We may avoid taking risks or trying new things when we fear failure. However, staying in our comfort zone limits our growth potential and keeps us from reaching our fullest potential.

When you understand the truth about failure, you become empowered to see it as a valuable part of your learning journey. Instead of avoiding failure, you can embrace it with courage and curiosity, using each experience to become better learners and achievers. The magic of failure lies in its valuable lessons, guiding you toward success and personal growth.

Real People Who Turned Failure into Success

> **Thomas Edison**, the brilliant inventor, is famous for his countless failures before successfully creating the electric lightbulb. He made over 1,000 unsuccessful attempts before achieving his breakthrough. Instead of getting discouraged, Edison famously declared that he had not failed but instead had found 1,000 ways it would not work. His perseverance and willingness to learn from each setback ultimately led to one of the most significant inventions in history.

> Before becoming a bestselling author in the Harry Potter series, **J.K. Rowling** faced numerous rejections from publishers. Her original manuscript for the first Harry Potter book was turned down twelve times, before it was finally accepted. However, she pursued her dream, and eventually, a small publisher took a chance on her. Her books have since sold millions of copies and inspired a generation of readers.

Michael Jordan, who is recognized as one of the world's greatest basketball player, faced numerous failures throughout his career. He missed over 9,000 shots and lost more than 300 games. Yet, he used each setback as motivation to work harder and improve his skills. Jordan once said, "*I've missed over 9,000 shots in my career. I've lost almost 300 games. 26 times, I've been trusted to take the game-winning shot and missed. I've failed over and over and over again in my life. And that is why I succeed.*" His journey reminds us that even the greatest achievers turn failures into stepping stones on their path to success.

The co-founder of Apple Inc., **Steve Jobs**, experienced a significant setback when he was fired from his own company in 1985. However, he didn't let this failure define him. Jobs continued to pursue his passion for innovation and went on to create Pixar Animation Studios and NeXT Inc. Eventually, he returned to Apple and played a pivotal role in revolutionizing the tech industry by introducing iconic products like the iPod, iPhone, and iPad.

Before becoming one of the most influential media moguls, **Oprah Winfrey** faced numerous challenges in her career. She was fired from her first TV job as an anchor and was told she was unfit for television. Undeterred, Oprah didn't let this failure stop her from pursuing her passion. She later found her way into talk shows, and her compassionate and engaging style resonated with audiences. Today, Oprah is a successful talk show host, philanthropist, actress, and media powerhouse.

These examples show that successful individuals like Thomas Edison, J.K. Rowling, Michael Jordan, Steve Jobs, and Oprah Winfrey embraced failure as a natural part of their journeys. They used setbacks as opportunities to learn, grow, and persevere, ultimately achieving greatness through determination, innovation, and resilience. Their stories are powerful reminders that failure is not the end but part of your path to success.

Embracing Feedback for Growth

Feedback guides us toward improvement and success. However, it can be challenging to hear, and nobody really likes to hear negative things about themselves. It can make us feel uncomfortable and even tempted to give up.

Feedback is simply information about how we're doing and where we can improve. Like a coach giving tips to a team, feedback helps us see our blind spots and discover areas for growth.

Nobody is perfect, and we all have things we can work on. Instead of seeing feedback as criticism, consider it an opportunity to become even better at what you do.

When you receive feedback, it's essential to keep an open mind. Sometimes, your first instinct might be to get defensive or ignore it, but that won't help you grow. Embrace feedback with curiosity and a desire to learn.

Remember, feedback is about your actions and performance, not your worth as a person. It doesn't define who you are.

As you work on the feedback and make improvements, celebrate your progress. Acknowledge your growth and pat yourself on the back for your efforts. Instead of feeling discouraged by feedback, use it as motivation to improve. Think of it as a challenge to overcome and a chance to become even better than before.

When seeking feedback, ask for specific and constructive comments. This helps you understand precisely what you can work on and how to improve.

Not all feedback may be helpful or relevant. Use your judgment to determine which feedback aligns with your goals and values. Over time, you will also learn how much value to place on the feedback, depending upon its source.

So, let's remember that embracing feedback is a superpower that can lead us to incredible success.

> It's like having a magic mirror that shows us where we shine and where we can sparkle even brighter.

Learning to Improve through Feedback

Learning to embrace feedback is like having a secret potion that helps you become the best version of yourself. So, let's discover how feedback can be your most valuable tool for progress and success.

Embrace the Growth Mindset

Embracing a growth mindset makes accepting feedback with an open heart easier. Feedback is always an opportunity to learn and grow, not judge your abilities. Embrace the belief that you can improve with effort and dedication.

Seek Feedback with Courage

Don't sit back and wait for feedback. If you really want to be the best version of yourself, you should ask for it from trusted sources. You may find asking for feedback intimidating, but it's a brave step towards growth. Approach teachers, mentors, or friends and ask for their input. You can say, "I'd love to hear your thoughts on improving. Your feedback means a lot to me."

Listen Actively

When receiving feedback, practice active listening. Pay attention to what's being said without interrupting or getting defensive. Take a moment to process the input before responding. In other words, listen to understand and not to respond. This is a skill that will benefit you in all aspects of your life.

Appreciate Positive Feedback

Positive feedback, although as valuable as constructive criticism, is always good to hear. Celebrate your strengths and accomplishments while also seeking areas for improvement. Remember, although feedback is about pointing out mistakes, it is also about acknowledging your progress.

Extract Actionable Insights

Look for specific and actionable insights in the feedback you receive. Focus on the areas where you can make tangible improvements. For example, if someone says you could improve your writing, ask for specific suggestions on enhancing your writing skills. When you focus on the specifics, your mind is focused on your success.

Learn from Mistakes

Don't be disheartened if feedback points out mistakes. Without this feedback, how will you know where you went wrong or what to improve or do differently next time?

Set Improvement Goals

Based on the feedback, set clear improvement goals for yourself. Break these goals into smaller steps and work on them one by one. It is a good idea to track your progress so you can celebrate each milestone achieved.

Be Patient and Persistent

Improving based on feedback takes time and effort. Be patient with yourself and stay persistent.

As you learn to improve through feedback, remember that it is a powerful personal growth and development tool. Embrace it with courage, seek it with an open mind, and use it to **unlock the door to your true potential**. You'll grow wiser, stronger, and more resilient with every step forward.

I believe you're now ready to discover the *Growth Mindset Superpowers*!

> *"A positive mindset creates positive actions,
> which lead to positive outcomes."*
> *- Anonymous*

Chapter 13

Growth Mindset Superpowers

Just like superheroes have unique powers, a growth mindset equips us with magical superpowers essential for personal growth that are vital for us to impact the world around us positively.

These Growth Mindset Superpowers are crucial for personal growth and success and essential for building a brighter, kinder, and more harmonious world.

If you've ever wished you had a superpower, it's time to discover that they've been inside you all the time.

With these qualities, you can positively influence those around you, lifting them with your courage, inspiring them with your creativity, and supporting them with empathy and resilience.

Together, let's unlock the magic within us and embrace the boundless potential of a growth mindset to create a better and more compassionate world for all.

So, what exactly are these superpowers?

When focusing on your growth mindset, the following three superpowers are key:

1. **Courage and Confidence**
2. **Creativity and Innovation**
3. **Empathy and Resilience**

Courage and Confidence

Courage and confidence are essential in embracing a growth mindset. They empower you to face challenges, conquer fears, and embrace new experiences with unwavering determination.

Remember, being courageous and brave doesn't mean being fearless. It means taking action even when you feel scared. Courage is a skill that can be developed with practice and determination.

Courage is like a shining light guiding you through dark times. With courage, you step outside your comfort zone and take bold steps toward your dreams. It helps you confront your fears, whether trying something new, speaking up, or standing up for what is right.

When we face challenges with courage, we unlock the doors to endless possibilities.

Confidence is the magic mirror that reflects your belief in yourself and your abilities. It is not about being perfect but about having faith in your potential if you make the effort to learn and grow.

When we cultivate self-confidence, we see challenges as opportunities for growth, knowing we have the inner strength to overcome obstacles.

Confidence reminds you that you are worthy and deserving of success and happiness. It encourages you to embrace your unique strengths and talents, recognizing that we all have something valuable to contribute to the world.

To be more courageous and brave, you can follow these steps:

Acknowledge Fear

The first step in building courage is acknowledging your fears. Instead of suppressing or denying them, recognize them and understand that it's okay to feel afraid.

By acknowledging your fears, you will be able to face them head-on.

Set Goals

Define clear and achievable goals, even if it means stepping out of your comfort zone. Break these goals into smaller, manageable steps.

Having a purpose and direction will motivate you to be brave in pursuing your objectives.

Take Small Steps

Take small steps outside your comfort zone. Gradually increase the difficulty as you become more comfortable with discomfort. Each step will build your confidence and make you more courageous over time.

Visualize Success

Imagine successfully facing your fears and achieving your goals. Visualization can boost your confidence and create a positive mindset, making you more prepared for challenges.

Challenge Negative Thoughts

Reframe negative thoughts that may hold you back from being courageous by replacing them with positive affirmations that reinforce your abilities and strengths.

Practice Self-Compassion

Be kind to yourself, especially when facing challenges. Treat yourself with the same kindness and understanding that you would show a friend. Acknowledge that being brave doesn't mean being perfect.

Celebrate Achievements

Always acknowledge and celebrate your brave actions and accomplishments, no matter how small they may seem. Celebrating your efforts will reinforce your courage and motivate you to take on more challenges.

Creativity and Innovation

Creativity is the magical spark that ignites your imagination and opens the door to new ideas. It's the ability to think outside the box, see things from different perspectives, and find innovative solutions. With creativity, ordinary situations can be turned into extraordinary adventures.

Curiosity is the key that unlocks the gates of creativity. Embrace your innate curiosity, ask questions, and explore the world with wonder. Curiosity leads to discoveries and fuels creativity.

Innovation is about using creativity to make a positive impact. Identify challenges or problems that matter to you, and use your creative powers to find solutions that can make a difference.

Surround yourself with inspiration from various sources, such as books, art, nature, or conversations. Inspiration sparks the creative fire within and helps you see the world freshly.

With the superpowers of creativity and innovation at your fingertips, you become the architect of your own magical world.

> *Embrace the wonders of creativity and innovation, and let your imagination take flight.*

Here are some practical exercises to experiment with creativity and innovation:

Idea Journal

Keep an idea journal where you jot down thoughts, ideas, or questions that come to mind throughout the day. Set aside a few minutes each day to brainstorm and explore these ideas further. This exercise will help you nurture your creativity and encourage innovative thinking.

Random Word Association

Here's a fun exercise to get your creativity flowing. Pick a random word from a dictionary or generate one using an online random word generator. Use this word as a starting point to brainstorm ideas, connections, or solutions. Let your imagination run wild and see where it takes you.

Picture Prompts

Find an interesting picture or artwork and use it as a creative prompt. Write a short story or poem, or draw a picture inspired by the image. This exercise will help you look at things differently and spark new ideas, which is an excellent problem-solving tool when you feel stuck.

Reverse Thinking

Take a problem or challenge you're facing and try to solve it in reverse. Instead of asking, "How do I solve this?" ask, "How do I make this problem worse?" Then, work backward to find innovative solutions to prevent those negative outcomes.

Mind Mapping

Create a mind map for a topic or project you're working on. Write the main idea in the center and branch out with related ideas and subtopics. Mind mapping helps organize thoughts, make connections, and stimulate creativity.

Role Play

Enact a scenario or situation from a different perspective or persona. This role-playing exercise can lead to fresh insights and innovative ideas you might not have considered before.

Build Something

Get hands-on by building a physical model or prototype of an idea or concept. Use craft materials, LEGO bricks, or any other available materials. Creating something tangible can unlock your creative potential and help you explore innovative designs.

Take a Break in Nature

Spend time to clear your mind and relax. Nature has a way of inspiring creativity and fostering innovative thinking. Take a walk, hike, or sit by a serene spot to let your mind wander and connect with your surroundings.

Think Beyond Limits

Break free from limitations and embrace limitless thinking. Challenge yourself to push boundaries, take risks, and venture into uncharted territory. With a growth mindset, there are no limits to what you can imagine.

Brainwriting

This is similar to brainstorming, but everyone writes down their thoughts on a topic or problem instead of sharing ideas. Then, pass the ideas around, and each person builds on the previous ones. This collaborative approach can lead to innovative and diverse solutions.

Nurture Playfulness

Embrace the playful spirit within you. Playfulness encourages you to experiment, try new things, and approach challenges with joy and curiosity. It opens the door to innovative thinking and unique solutions.

Collaborate and Share

Collaborate with others and share your creative ideas. Collaboration sparks the fusion of diverse perspectives, leading to even more innovative and groundbreaking outcomes.

Explore New Fields

Delve into areas of knowledge or interests you have yet to explore. Read books, watch documentaries, or take online courses on subjects outside your comfort zone. Expanding your understanding can spark new ideas and cross-pollinate creativity.

> Remember, there's no right or wrong way to be creative and innovative. The key is experimenting, playing, and having fun with these exercises. Be open to exploring new ideas by stepping out of your comfort zone.

With a growth mindset, you'll find that creativity and innovation become powerful tools to unleash your full potential and unlock the magic of limitless possibilities so that you can grow into the best version of yourself.

Empathy and Resilience

Like compassionate guides on our journey, empathy and resilience accompany us as we embrace a growth mindset. These superpowers will enrich your life, helping you forge meaningful connections with others and navigate through life's challenges with grace and strength, and should never be underrated.

The Gift of Empathy

Empathy is the ability to show understanding of how another person feels. It is like having a magic mirror that reflects the emotions and experiences of those around us.

With empathy, you can step into the shoes of others, offering kindness, support, and compassion. It fosters a sense of belonging and a caring community.

The Strength of Resilience

Resilience is your superpower to bounce back from challenges and setbacks. It's like a magical shield that protects you from despair and gives you the strength to rise after falling. Resilience helps you face adversity with courage and determination.

With the superpowers of empathy and resilience, you become a pillar of support for yourself and others. Embrace the magic of empathy, connecting with others on a deeper level. Harness the strength of resilience, rising above difficulties and emerging stronger than before.

> *As you cultivate these superpowers, you create a nurturing and empathetic world around you and discover the inner strength to weather any storm.*

Follow the tips below to harness these superpowers:

Reframe Challenges

Instead of seeing challenges as insurmountable obstacles, view them as opportunities for growth and learning. Reframe negative thoughts into positive ones that promote resilience.

The more you work at this, the easier it will become.

Active Listening

Practice active listening to understand what others are going through. Please give them your full attention without judgment or interruption. When you listen with empathy, you create a safe space for others to express themselves openly.

Practice Perspective-Taking

Put yourself in the shoes of others and try to see the world from their point of view. This exercise builds empathy and helps you better understand diverse experiences and feelings.

Acts of Kindness

Perform acts of kindness towards others, whether offering a helping hand, a warm smile, or a word of encouragement. Even small acts of kindness can bring hope and happiness and create a ripple effect of positivity, as kindness is an act that keeps on giving.

Practice Empathetic Body Language

Use open body language, maintain eye contact, and offer comforting gestures like nodding or a gentle touch when appropriate. These nonverbal cues are important because they show that you are present and attentive, and you are more likely to build trust by doing this.

Develop Problem-Solving Skills

Focus on finding solutions rather than dwelling on the problems. Approach obstacles with a proactive and solution-oriented mindset.

Focus On Solutions

Get into the habit of focusing on finding solutions instead of dwelling on problems. Resilience is about adapting and persevering in the face of challenges, knowing you have the strength to overcome them.

Ask Open-Ended Questions

Asking open-ended questions encourages others to share their thoughts and feelings. Open-ended questions are questions that can't be answered with a simple yes or no. Using words like how, what, where, when, and why in your questions create open-ended questions. This helps others express themselves more freely and allows you to gain deeper insights into their experiences.

.Be Non-Judgmental

Avoid making assumptions or judgments about other people's feelings or experiences. Create a safe space where they can be open without fear of criticism by always treating others how you would like to be treated.

Learn from Adversity

Reflect on past experiences of resilience and growth. Recognize how you have overcome challenges and draw strength from those experiences.

Set Realistic Goals

Break down larger goals into smaller, achievable steps. Celebrate each milestone as you progress, boosting your confidence and resilience.

Remember that practicing empathy and resilience is an ongoing journey. Developing these superpowers takes time and effort, but **the rewards are immeasurable**.

> *With a growth mindset, empathy, and resilience, you'll navigate life's challenges gracefully, build meaningful connections, and positively impact yourself and those around you.*

Embrace all these superpowers, and let them guide you toward personal growth and well-being.

Let's continue your growth mindset adventure by taking everything you've learned to the next level in the following chapter, *Continuing Your Magic Mindset Adventure*.

> *"You are capable of far more than you know.
> Don't limit yourself."*
> \- Unknown

Chapter 14

Continuing Your Mindset Magic Adventure

As you approach the end of your Mindset Magic adventure, it is essential to understand the significance of continuity and why this adventure is more than just a one-time experience.

This final chapter delves into the lifelong impact of embracing a growth mindset. This journey is not bound by time. It is about making a lifelong commitment to growth and learning that can transform your life in remarkable ways.

Throughout this book, you've unlocked the secrets of growth mindset superpowers, learned to conquer challenges, and embraced the transformational magic of resilience, empathy, and creativity. Now, as we near the end of this adventure, it's essential to recognize that the journey of a growth mindset doesn't end here - **it's a lifetime ambition**.

Continuing your magic mindset adventure means making a lasting commitment to lifelong learning. The world constantly changes, and there is always something new to discover. With a growth mindset, you'll approach each day as another chance to learn and grow, regardless of age or circumstances.

Life is a series of adventures, and with a growth mindset, you'll embrace each experience as a chance to become the best version of yourself. This commitment to personal growth will empower you to seize opportunities to overcome challenges that come your way.

Resilience is another critical aspect of this journey. Life may present obstacles and setbacks, but with a growth mindset, you'll face them with resilience and determination. You'll bounce back from adversity, knowing failures are stepping stones to success.

Cultivating curiosity will be an integral part of your adventure. Embrace a sense of wonder and curiosity about the world. This curiosity will drive you to explore, ask questions, and seek new experiences, leading to continuous growth and transformation.

Accepting challenges will be an essential part of your journey, too. Challenges are not roadblocks but invitations to grow and learn. With a growth mindset, you'll welcome challenges as opportunities for self-improvement and self-discovery.

Ultimately, you become the author of your own magical story. With a growth mindset, you create your narrative and shape a life filled with purpose, passion, and fulfillment.

Embrace the power of continuity, for it is through continuous learning and growth that you'll unlock the true magic within yourself. Make this journey a lifetime ambition, and watch as your life unfolds into an extraordinary tale of courage, perseverance, and limitless potential.

As your magic mindset adventure continues, you'll create an enchanting life with it.

Spreading Magic to Others

Share what you've discovered by embracing the spirit of sharing and spreading the magic of a growth mindset to others. Just as a candle doesn't lose its flame by lighting another, your magic mindset grows even brighter as you empower and inspire those around you.

Be an Empowering Role Model

Put everything you've learned into practice and lead by example to showcase the power of a growth mindset in your own life. Demonstrate resilience, curiosity, and a willingness to embrace challenges, inspiring others to follow suit.

Share Your Story

Openly share your growth mindset journey with others. Discuss the challenges you faced, what you changed, and the lessons you learned to experience your personal growth. Explain how you overcame challenges and the difference you experienced in your outcome by having a growth mindset. Your story can ignite hope and motivation in others to embark on their own Mindset Magic adventure.

Encourage a Growth Mindset

Whenever you notice someone struggling or feeling defeated, offer encouragement and support. Remind them of the power of a growth mindset and how challenges can be transformed into opportunities for growth. Again, this is an excellent opportunity to use your own experiences to encourage this.

Foster Empathy and Understanding

Practice empathy by genuinely listening to others and acknowledging their feelings. Understand that everyone's journey is unique and may be at a different stage of embracing a growth mindset. Remember, there is a fine balance between offering advice and coming across as a know-it-all, so always be mindful of this.

Celebrate Effort and Progress

Praise others for their efforts and progress, regardless of the outcome. Celebrate the journey and the hard work, reinforcing that growth is continuous and rewarding.

Create a Supportive Environment

Foster an environment where people feel safe to take risks and embrace challenges. Encourage an environment of growth and learning where mistakes are seen as opportunities for improvement.

Offer Feedback and Constructive Criticism

When giving feedback, make sure it's constructive by focusing on specific areas for improvement and growth rather than criticizing individuals. Provide constructive feedback that encourages them to learn and develop their skills, and always remember to focus on the positive too.

Collaborate and Share Knowledge

Engage in collaborative learning experiences and share knowledge. Collaboration fuels growth and empowers everyone involved to learn from each other's unique perspectives.

Lead with Gratitude

Show appreciation to those who have supported and encouraged you on your growth mindset journey. Gratitude is contagious and reminds us of the positive impact we can have on each other's lives.

> *By spreading the magic of a growth mindset to others, you become a catalyst for positive change and transformation.*

As you empower those around you, you contribute to a ripple effect of growth, resilience, and continuous learning in your community and beyond.

Be excited about the opportunity to make a difference.

Let your magic mindset shine brightly, illuminating the path for others to embrace their enchanting journey of growth and self-discovery.

Embracing a Lifetime of Growth

Your journey has no endpoint. It's a constant exploration and development path. Committing to a lifetime of growth means committing to the magic of learning, evolving, and becoming the best version of yourself every step of the way.

Set Lifelong Goals

As you continue your adventure, set meaningful and achievable goals for yourself. Whether they involve personal growth, professional success, or positively impacting others, having plans to work towards provides direction and purpose.

Seek New Experiences

Look for the magic of new experiences and opportunities. Travel to new places, engage in different hobbies and leave your comfort zone. Each experience broadens your horizons and enriches your understanding of the world.

Learn from Everyone

Accept the diversity of perspectives around you. Everyone you encounter has something valuable to offer, and you can learn from their experiences, insights, and wisdom. Be open to continuous learning from all walks of life.

Reflect and Learn from Challenges

As you face challenges, reflect on the lessons they bring. Analyze your experiences, identify areas for improvement, and use setbacks as catalysts for growth.

Never Stop Questioning

Curiosity is the driving force behind a lifetime of growth. Keep asking questions, seeking answers, and exploring the unknown. Curiosity fuels your desire to learn and discover the magic beyond what you already know.

Embrace Continuous Learning

Formal education is just one part of the learning journey. Embrace opportunities for continuous learning through reading, watching documentaries, attending workshops, online courses, or engaging in discussions with others.

Surround Yourself with Growth-Oriented People

Seek the company of individuals who share your passion for growth and learning. Surrounding yourself with growth-oriented people creates a supportive environment that encourages personal development.

Celebrate Your Growth

Acknowledge and celebrate your progress on your Magic Mindset adventure. Each step forward, no matter how small, is a testament to your commitment to growth. Embrace your accomplishments and use them as motivation to keep moving forward.

Embracing a lifetime of growth is an awe-inspiring and fulfilling journey. It is a commitment to evolving into the best version of yourself and discovering the enchanting possibilities that await.

> *Remember, there is no end to the magic of learning and self-discovery. With every chapter in your life story, you'll uncover new strengths, insights, and opportunities for growth.*

Step confidently into the unknown, embrace the magic of continuity, and let your lifetime of growth be a testament to the extraordinary potential that resides within you.

You Are the Master of Your Mindset Journey

To become the master of your mindset journey, start by cultivating self-awareness. Reflect on your thoughts, emotions, and reactions to different situations. Understand your strengths, areas for growth, and the beliefs that influence your mindset. Choose thoughts that empower and uplift you.

Whenever negative or self-limiting thoughts arise, dismiss them and replace these thoughts with positive affirmations that reinforce your growth mindset.

Be kind to yourself in your inner dialogue. Encourage and support yourself just as you would a friend. The way you speak to yourself profoundly impacts your mindset and self-esteem.

Embrace the word "YET" as your magical ally. Add "YET" to the end of your sentences when faced with challenges or setbacks. This small word opens up possibilities and keeps you focused on growth.

Practice mindfulness, allowing you to stay present, observe your thoughts, and choose how to respond. By staying mindful, you can catch any negative thought patterns before they take hold and consciously redirect your focus toward positive perspectives.

Be intentional about your mindset journey. Set clear intentions for what you want to achieve and the mindset you wish to cultivate. Break down these intentions into actionable goals and steps to track your progress.

Always view challenges as opportunities for growth. Seek new experiences, learning opportunities, and moments to step out of your comfort zone. Each challenge you conquer strengthens your growth mindset.

Remember that even masters need mentors to seek support and guidance from individuals who inspire them and embody a growth mindset. Their insights and encouragement can be invaluable on your journey.

Embrace the flexibility of your mindset journey. Allow yourself to adapt and evolve as you learn and grow. Flexibility enables you to navigate through life's changes with grace and resilience.

Celebrate every milestone and achievement along your journey. Recognize your growth and acknowledge the effort you put in.

Celebrations fuel motivation and keep you enthusiastic about the following chapters of your adventure.

Believe you hold the key to unlocking the magic within your mindset. As the master of your mindset journey, you can transform your beliefs, rewrite your story, and design a life filled with enchanting growth and boundless possibilities.

> *Action this newfound power, as it is the start of a lifetime of continuous learning and becoming the hero of your magical story.*

The adventure is yours to embrace, and the magic of a growth mindset awaits you, ready to illuminate every step of your journey.

"The journey of a thousand miles begins with a single step."
- Lao Tzu

Conclusion

Throughout this book, we've explored the belief that we can learn, improve, and achieve our goals with effort and determination over time with a mindset of growth.

You learned to acknowledge your efforts and achievements, and I congratulate you on making it to the end of this book. I know you might not have always found it easy, but I hope your effort has left you feeling good about yourself and confident about your future.

So, well done!

By embracing a growth mindset, you've learned that challenges are not roadblocks but opportunities for growth and learning. You've discovered your unique superpowers—courage, confidence, creativity, innovation, empathy, and resilience, which will help you face obstacles with bravery and optimism throughout your life.

You've embraced challenges with courage, unlocked your creativity to find innovative solutions, showed empathy towards others, and bounced back stronger from setbacks. These superpowers have empowered you to face life's ups and downs with confidence and determination.

Along this adventure, you've made valuable connections with others who share your passion for growth and learning. Supporting and inspiring each other, you've created a network of encouragement beyond the pages of this book.

As we conclude this magical lesson, remember you shape your mindset journey. Your thoughts and attitudes can unlock the magic within you, leading to a life filled with wonder and endless possibilities. Embrace the magic of a growth mindset, as it will guide you through a lifetime of learning to become the best version of yourself.

As you complete this book, know that the adventure doesn't end here. Embrace the essence of continuity and approach each day with a growth mindset. Embrace challenges, seek new opportunities to learn, and celebrate your progress. Each day presents an opportunity to grow and develop regardless of age or circumstances. You've learned to be open-minded, seek out new experiences, and approach life with curiosity and enthusiasm.

Thank you for joining me on this magical adventure. As you continue your journey, remember that you can create a life filled with wonder, courage, and endless possibilities.

I hope you embrace the magic within and let your growth mindset be the guiding star that lights your path to a bright and fulfilling future.

Our adventure together may have concluded, but the magic of a growth mindset will accompany you wherever you go. May you always approach life with curiosity, determination, and the knowledge that you are the hero of your own story.

With courage in your heart, creativity in your mind, empathy in your actions, and resilience in your spirit, you can create a lifetime of growth to fulfill your potential beyond your wildest dreams.

> *The magic of a growth mindset awaits you, ready to illuminate every step of your lifelong adventure. The world is your playground, and with a growth mindset, there are no limits to what you can achieve.*

You are the author of your story, the master of your mindset, and the hero of your magical journey. So go forth, my young friend, and let the magic of a growth mindset be your compass on this extraordinary journey called life.

> *"The greatest glory in living lies not in never falling, but in rising every time we fall."*
> *- Nelson Mandela*

Which Door Will You Open?

As you begin this fun section, get ready to put your growth mindset knowledge into practice. You'll encounter a series of scenarios, each presenting you with choices that reflect what you've learned about having a growth mindset.

Imagine walking through a door to your choice. Before walking through the door, choose which door to open by selecting your choice from the available options. Embrace this opportunity to showcase your understanding and put your magical superpowers into action.

Remember, a growth mindset empowers you to view challenges as opportunities and setbacks as stepping stones to success. It's about believing in your ability to learn, improve, and grow, no matter the circumstances. With each scenario, choose the response that aligns with the magic of a growth mindset.

Each scenario has three options. Just as in real life, some options will not serve you well, and others will bring you closer to achieving your goals. Some may be similar. There are no correct answers here. So, choose the option that is right for you now.

I am not going to check your choices. To get the most out of this exercise, be honest with yourself and give some thought to each choice you make.

Are you ready to reveal the depths of your growth mindset magic? Then, let's embark on this fun exercise, where your choices will showcase how much you have grown.

You've been trying to learn a new skill but keep making mistakes. What do you do?

    1. Give up and try something else.

    2. Keep practicing and learning from your mistakes.

    3. Seek help from a mentor or teacher to improve.

You receive feedback on a project you worked hard on, and it's not as positive as you hoped. How do you react?

    1. Feel discouraged and believe you're not good enough.

    2. Use the feedback to improve as a growth opportunity.

    3. Share your project with others to get their views and ideas.

You encounter a challenging Math problem that seems too difficult to solve. What's your approach?

    1. Avoid the problem and move on to something easier.

    2. Embrace the challenge, seek help, and work at it.

    3. Break the problem down into smaller parts.

Your friend is better at a sport than you are, making you feel inadequate. What do you do?

1. Compare yourself to your friend and feel defeated.

2. Appreciate your friend's skills and use them as motivation to improve your own abilities.

3. Ask your friend for tips and practice together.

You've been practicing playing an instrument but still struggle with specific notes. What's your attitude?

1. Give up because you believe you'll never get better.

2. Keep practicing, as improvement takes time and effort.

3. Find a music tutor or join a group to receive guidance.

You receive a low grade on a test. How do you handle it?

1. Believe you're not smart enough and give up on studying.

2. Use the grade as feedback to identify areas for improvement and study harder next time.

3. Talk to your teacher to understand your mistakes and ask for guidance.

You have a big presentation coming up, and you feel nervous. How do you cope?

1. Avoid the presentation because you're afraid of failing and don't feel comfortable being the focus of attention.

2. Acknowledge your nerves and practice to build confidence in your abilities so you feel capable.

3. Share your nervousness with a friend or family member for support and encouragement.

You're trying to solve a complex problem, and it's taking longer than expected. What's your response?

1. Get frustrated and give up and go and do something fun.

2. See the challenge as an opportunity to build and improve your problem-solving skills and persist until you find a solution.

3. Collaborate with others to brainstorm ideas and work together towards a solution.

You made a mistake in a group project, and your teammates are upset. What do you decide to do?

1. Blame others for the mistake and distance yourself from the project.

2. Take responsibility for the mistake, apologize, and work together to find a solution.

3. Organize a meeting with your group to address the issue, understand each other's perspectives, and find a resolution.

You're working on a school project, and your group members aren't cooperating. What do you do?

1. Do the whole project by yourself, feeling frustrated with your group.

2. Communicate with your group, find ways to work together, and resolve any conflicts constructively.

3. Talk to your teacher about the situation and ask for advice on improving teamwork.

A growth mindset means deciding on the responses that foster growth, learning, and resilience. Embrace the power of your mindset, and you'll unlock a world of endless possibilities and magical achievements!

Always remember, choosing the growth mindset option will help you make the most of every magical opportunity that comes your way!

As you progress through life, which doors will you choose to open?

> *"Every accomplishment starts with the decision to try."*
> - John F. Kennedy

Glossary

adversity: hardship or a troubling situation

affirmations: statements that promote positive thinking

belittles: to make someone feel they aren't important

boundless: unlimited; having no limits

catalyst: an event or person that causes a change

composure: feeling calm, in control and confident

concept: a thought or idea

constructive criticism: feedback that offers suggestions for improvement

counteract: to reduce or remove the effect of something

cultivate: to nurture and help grow

dedication: committing to something

demeanor: outward manner or behavior

destiny: a future that includes something great or important

dialogue: an exchange of words; a conversation

diligently: a thoughtful and devoted effort

dispel: remove or drive away

essence: the most meaningful element of a person or thing

feedback: information given to someone on what they've said or done

foes: enemies

formidable: something that causes fear, dread or worry

fostering: encouraging development or growth in something

grace: behave in a pleasant and dignified way

hinder: prevent the progress of something

impact: a major effect on something or someone

inadequacy: something that is not enough

incantations: magical words that are sung or spoken

indomitable: unconquerable, difficult to defeat or frighten

inevitable: unable to be avoided

infuse: to introduce or encourage something (with)

inhibits: to prevent or hold back from something

integral: the main part

limitations: a restrictive condition; inability

malleability: the ability to be easily changed into a new shape

manifest: evidence of something appearing or happening

mentors: role models offering guidance

narrative: the story

optimism: thinking positively

perseverance: ability to keep doing something in spite of obstacles

persistence: not giving up, continue to strive for something

perspective: the way you see something

pessimistic: thinking negatively

phoenix rising from ashes: a bird going through rebirth; starting over

proficiency: to have an above-average skill in something

profound: feeling or experiencing something in a strong way

reciprocity: the exchange of something between people

resilient: ability to withstand setbacks and bounce back

resonate: to mean something to someone close to their values or beliefs

self-compassion: treating yourself kindly when things don't go well

self-criticism: evaluating yourself negatively, saying harsh things to yourself

self-empowerment: taking charge of your life

self-image: how you see and what you think about yourself

sage: a wise person or philosopher

shortcomings: weaknesses

steadfastness: something that is steady or fixed

strategies: plans intended to achieve something

stress: a state of worry

tension: a feeling of anxiety that makes you unable to relax

testament: a statement of belief

traits: a character feature

trajectory: a path or direction of a person or something

transformative: ability to cause a major change

unconsciously: not aware, do something automatically without thought

unyielding: being stubborn or not giving way

validity: being based on truth

vital: necessary or essential

worthiness: deserving respect, praise or attention

"Attitude is a little thing that makes a big difference."
- Winston Churchill

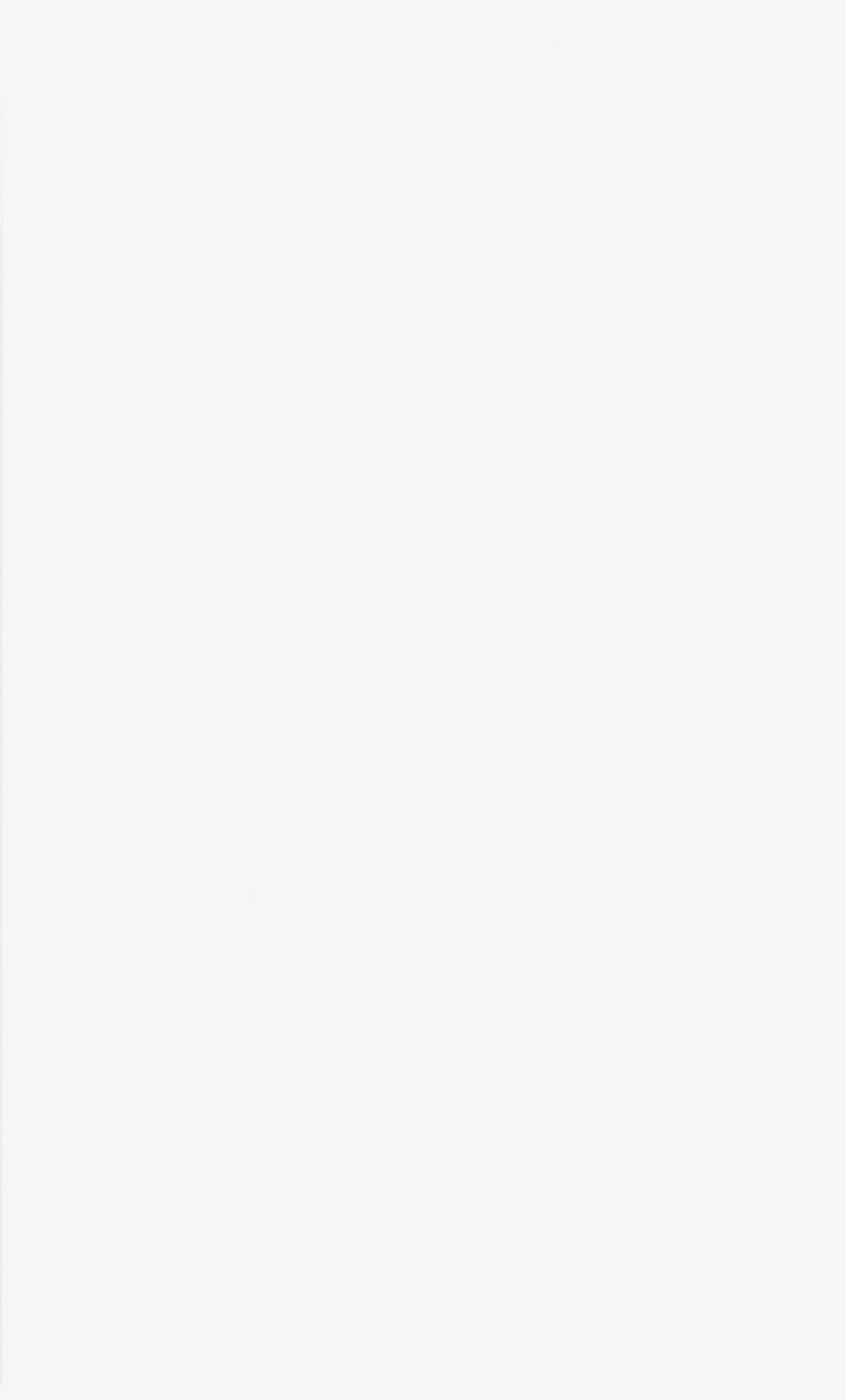

www.ingramcontent.com/pod-product-compliance
Lightning Source LLC
Chambersburg PA
CBHW021109080526
44587CB00010B/450